Hiding *Boys* in *Bathrooms*

A Decade of Dating Debacles

GIULIANA PRADA

authorHOUSE®

AuthorHouse™
1663 Liberty Drive
Bloomington, IN 47403
www.authorhouse.com
Phone: 1 (800) 839-8640

© *2017 Cover Artwork by Andrea Simons*
www.andreamichellesimons.com

Published by AuthorHouse   03/21/2017

ISBN: 978-1-5246-6859-4 (sc)
ISBN: 978-1-5246-6860-0 (hc)
ISBN: 978-1-5246-6858-7 (e)

Library of Congress Control Number: 2017901077

Print information available on the last page.

This book is printed on acid-free paper.

Contents

And another one bites the dust
But why can I not conquer love?

And I want it and I wanted it bad
But there were so many red flags …

—Sia, "Elastic Heart"

For Mom

The Blunder Years

blun•der

n. a serious or embarrassing mistake, usually the result of carelessness
or ignorance

v. 1. to make a serious or embarrassing mistake as a result of carelessness
or ignorance

2. to stumble or move clumsily

3. to act in a manner that is clumsy, ignorant, or thoughtless

Little did I know, as I embarked upon my freshman year of college, that
my blunderdom was just about to begin, big-time.

I'm not even necessarily talking about the noticeable drop in my
grade point average, although that did cause my mother a considerable
amount of disturbance. No, I'm talking about alcohol and boys. I
couldn't have known then, but from that point on, the two would quite
often be intertwined, somewhat in my twenties but especially in my
thirties. Let me clarify that by the time I'd reached my thirties, they
were no longer boys. They were pretty much men—but men who mostly
acted like boys.

However, first came alcohol, although it took a while for me to latch
onto that vice. By all sense of the term, I am a late bloomer in just about
every aspect of my life. You name it, and I will do it, but about five to
ten years later than everyone else I know. For example, after graduating
from college, while all my friends were busy apartment hunting in
trendy San Francisco neighborhoods like the Marina and Russian Hill,
I was perfectly content living at home. I could visit my friends in the city
anytime I wanted to enjoy a night up there. I didn't need to live there.

Ten or so years later, as most of my friends married and moved back to the burbs, I moved to the city. Of course, it was the Sunset District, close to the beach and basically far away from what anybody else in the city deemed cool and hip, but I had finally done it. My friends were shocked and very concerned, mostly about where to send my Christmas cards. Would I really be staying there long, in (technically) the city? They all scratched their heads in wonder. I'd blown their minds, and I was actually kind of enjoying it. Of course, I threw them for a loop again when I moved home about a year later. Yeah, let's just say I've always had a slight problem with change. Unless it's a pair of kick-ass shoes, it can take me literally years to ease into something new. "What! High school's over? But I was just starting to really, actually like it." *Sigh.* Time to start all over again.

Anyway, you catch my drift on the whole late bloomer issue. The same applied to alcohol. I never touched the stuff in high school. In actuality, I was scared shitless of alcohol and drugs. The antidrug and antialcohol lessons that were somehow craftily tied to the "dangers of premarital sex" talk that they gave us in seventh grade at St. Dymphna's had done a successful doozy of a job on me.

First, we were given a paper—a narcotics study sheet, if you will—that listed all illegal drugs, their street names, and the ill effects of taking these substances, as well as the evils of alcohol, to be quizzed on, of course, at a later date. The drugs that particularly freaked me out were LSD and PCP, since, according to the narcotics sheet, people who took these drugs got super crazy-violent, hallucinated that bugs were crawling on them, and eventually threw themselves out windows or jumped to their deaths from roofs trying to fly. Note to seventh-grade self: *never* take drugs, especially LSD and PCP! And stay away from all parties in which some illegal substance can be slipped into your alcoholic drink (that you, of course, should most certainly not be drinking) or your food, causing you to go insanely paranoid or turn to prostitution to support your newfound drug/alcohol habit. And remember (so said the narcotics guide) that marijuana is the "gateway drug," the drug that leads to all others! Yes, I was completely paranoid, and I hadn't even taken any drugs.

As if that weren't scary enough, we had to watch some after-school-type special starring the former Marcia Brady of *Brady Bunch* fame titled "When Jenny? When?" Marcia (a.k.a. Jenny) played a sought-after high school gal with whom all the boys wanted to have sex. Apparently, they'd heard she was loose, and her reputation preceded her. Everywhere she went—parties, the school bleachers, some guy's van (he was supposedly giving her a ride home)—she was cornered by these guys and hounded about having sex with them. It was awful. But I'm not sure which was more disturbing to shy, sheltered seventh-grade me: (1) the actual topic of premarital sex with boys who wore cords, had slightly feathered hair, and drove creepy white vans or (2) the fact that Marcia Brady was playing the part of the harassed high school hussy, Jenny. I was just glad I wasn't named Jenny, like my best friend, who for the rest of the school year had to listen to the perverted boys in our class tease, "When, Jenny? When?"

As a result of being scared to death by Marcia, LSD, and any type of alcohol, I was not a big proponent of frequenting high school keggers where, with the exception of Marcia, I might come into contact with any of the devil's other accessories. In fact, I didn't go to any parties, always feigning I was "busy." I'm not sure whether anyone believed me, but, hey, the less the party crowd or anyone else really knew about me, the better.

In the social stratosphere of my all-girl Catholic high school, I was perfectly situated smack in the middle. I was neither an outcast dork nor a member of the upper-echelon, popular partier crowd. I was no extreme; I kept to my friends, who were fairly normal as well, and most people liked me. However, I knew that if I ever attended some party and politely declined an alcoholic beverage, pot, or the sloppy sexual advances of some intoxicated guy (assuming there would be some), my secret of being an abnormal high schooler would be out, and I would forever be regarded by all as an old-fashioned, boring prude. Instead, I opted to stay home and catch up on TV. I believe *MacGyver* was a Saturday-night favorite for quite some time, since dreamy Kirk Cameron of *Growing Pains* was only on Tuesday nights.

Suffice it to say, in my freshman year of college, my rigid no-drinking rule was once and for all shattered. I'm pretty sure it all started with the red jungle juice at a fraternity Halloween party. Take one utterly shy and awkward freshman, put her in a dark and crowded basement, blare

"Love Shack" by the B-52s repeatedly, and shove a drink in her hand, and alcohol and I were destined to become good friends sooner or later.

And it was downhill from there. When I say downhill, I don't mean I instantaneously turned into a raging alcoholic who never went to class (although those 8:30 a.m. anthropology classes certainly became much less appealing), but let's just say I was making up for lost time with the binge drinking and puking my guts up every weekend (and some weeknights) in the process. However, in the grand scheme of college life, I was actually pretty normal (so I thought) and fitting in quite nicely, even with the automatic puking reflex.

Now that I'd officially gotten my drink on, it was only a matter of time before my random encounters with boys would begin.

We all remember that old saying: "Sweet sixteen and never been kissed." Well, I was nineteen. Right, see previous references to being a late bloomer. Anyway, I know loads of people look back on that first kiss with fond nostalgia, as a magical and innocent rite of passage. "Ah, yes, summer vacation … Mark took me on a drive to show me the lights of Sunset Harbor, and then we kissed on that grassy knoll behind the cabins … I wonder whatever happened to Mark …" (insert girlish giggle and wistful sigh).

Others grimace and recoil with shame while recalling the painful awkwardness of it all. "Oh God, it was so *awful*. We both had braces, and then he completely slobbered all over me!" Wretched gagging sounds to follow. And then there are those of us who can't remember the kiss— because we were, uh, *slightly* intoxicated. Well, okay, I remember it, but with a tinge of fuzziness.

James lived on my dorm floor. He was a white guy from Seattle. I only mention that he was white because when he spoke, he sounded black. I know, weird, but apparently he had grown up in a black neighborhood. If you closed your eyes, you'd swear you were talking to Smokey Robinson or one of the members of Bell Biv Devoe. When I did get close enough to actually converse with him, I didn't mind. As you'll come to find out, I seem to have a thing for men with accents.

Anyway, he had a soft sort of drawl and quite a body, witnessed by all when he walked around in his typical outfit of long basketball shorts and a wifebeater. Oh, and get this—he liked me, or so everyone on my floor (girls and guys alike) would tell me. "Dude, he has a total crush on you! He thinks you're totally hot!" What? Somebody thought I was hot? That was a first.

As novel and flattering as that was, though, I was not about to let that go to my self-deprecating little head. Besides, I had zero romantic experience, and the thought of anything ever happening completely freaked me out. Because then the ugly truth would be out: I had no game . I was a no-gamer for sure. I mean, what the hell would I ever do with a boy? I had no idea.

Therefore, I became quite prone to jumping into open dorm rooms of friends if I even so much as caught a glimpse of James heading my way. *Oh my God, what am I going to do if he smiles at me again and starts talking to me with his Bell Biv Devoe voice? Oh God, what if he asks me out? Damn it, why does he have to like me?* A little dramatic, you say? I quite agree. It got to the ridiculous point where James's supposed crush on me and my continual dodging of him (as if he were that pesky Pepé Le Pew instead of the cute guy whom he was) became the dorm floor's running joke.

Then one Saturday afternoon, I decided to do something about this James situation. My friends and I were partaking in Sigma Pi's annual Reggae Sunsplash party. Reggae Sunsplash was basically a bunch of frat guys blasting Bob Marley on their stereo while we all stood around kegs, pounding beers in the sun. It was probably an excuse for a lot of weed smoking too, but remember that I'm scared of drugs. I stoically stuck to the keg—and for quite some time.

When we could drink no more beer because there was no more beer left, we all headed back to our dorm rooms to crash for a few hours before heading out again for the night. As I stood at my door, key in hand, I looked down the hallway. James's door was closed. Was he there? A sudden thought occurred in my hazy, beer-sloshed mind. Maybe I could just go down and knock and say hi, and if he wasn't there, no problem. If he was there, well, I would take matters into my own hands and end this silly nonsense. What harm could there be in some lighthearted chitchat? I mean, I would just go down to say hello and good-bye. That would certainly be fine. Sure, why not? *A perfectly good idea*, I thought, as many people do about most of their drinking-affiliated ideas.

Except I knew that while James and I might very well chitchat, he was also going to kiss me. I just knew it. He liked me, and I knew it. The whole floor knew it. It was inevitable that it was going to happen. It was wrong to prey on the vulnerability of another, even if he was a (probably horny) male, wasn't it? Yes, yes, it was. However, I was going to do it anyway, especially when I had all the liquid courage I needed. It was time to get this first kiss/make-out session over with—and before I sobered up too much and changed my mind.

I lurched down the hallway and hoped that James wasn't opposed to girls who smelled like breweries and secondhand pot smoke. However, by the time I reached the door, my courage had completely fled me. This was a stupid, stupid idea. What was I thinking? Yet, I knocked anyway, but all the while praying he wasn't there. *Yes!* Nobody was answering. I turned to hurry down the hallway, and that's when the door opened. I sincerely hoped it was his roommate.

"Hey, Giuliana ! What's up?" I heard his soft Bell Biv Devoe–like voice say. I turned around and saw James smiling, genuinely smiling at me.

"Oh, uh, nothing. Just came by to … say hi," I said lamely. The likelihood of my just "stopping by" to say hi was about as likely as my strolling down the hall naked. Anyone could've figured that out. I'm fairly sure it was obvious that this was my lame way of flirting with him. So far, James didn't seem to mind.

"Cool, I'm just studying. I could use a break. Come on in." He held the door open wide and waved me in.

I came in, he closed the door, and I don't remember much else. Well, I mean, we did talk. I don't have the vaguest recollection of what we talked about, except for a random conversation on various hip-hop and soul artists inspired by the fact that James happened to be playing his favorite Big Daddy Kane cassette tape. And then we kissed for a while. No fireworks went off. There were no shooting stars overhead. No trumpets sounded—just Big Daddy Kane playing softly in the background. But more importantly, there was no real awfulness, at least not for me. I can't vouch for poor James. Who knows what trauma he endured? And then I'm pretty sure I passed out.

When I woke up, it was dark. Don't worry, I was fully clothed. Unlike me, James did not try to take advantage of someone in a vulnerable (i.e., in my case, passed-out) state. James was asleep (and clothed too, just so you know), and I was unfortunately *very* sober. I was instantly mortified at my drunken boldness. There would be no cuddling—no, sir! I snuck out in a panic over what I had done. I was a brazen hussy! A tramp! What if James told everyone on the floor? I was in full-on paranoid mode.

I hid out for the good part of the week, furtively sneaking in and out of my dorm room in ninja-like style to get to and from classes. When the weekend came around, I went straight home under the guise of being homesick, just to get away from campus. I didn't want to run into James or to chance drinking too much and then stopping by for another visit to him. I mean, who knew what would happen with a drunken trollop like me?

When I returned to school I found a note that had been slipped under my door while I was away. It was from James. He wondered how I was. He hadn't seen me around much, and he asked if I wanted to do something that weekend. I was surprised and quite taken aback with happiness. So, I hadn't repulsed him with my Eau de Coors Light fragrance. And then, just as suddenly, I was completely put off with disgust. Of course, I didn't want to **do** anything! What did he think I was, some kind of a slut? I was obviously very conflicted, very *afflicted*. *Poor me. Poor, poor James.*

I never responded to his note. In fact, we never spoke again, at least for the rest of that freshman year. Eventually, we just began to avoid each other or to pretend we were not in the same vicinity of each other, even if we were. If I could go back in time, I'd like to apologize to James for being such a complete tool. He couldn't have known he was the first person to actually kiss me and what a young nineteen-year-old I really was.

James ended up being roommates with my good friend Tom our sophomore year, so I eventually talked to him, since I frequently came over to visit Tom. But by that time I was in a much safer place. And James was dating someone else. And by then, I was also dating … *Dante.*

Girlfriend in a Coma

Dante Prosecco—that was his name. Actually, that wasn't really his name, but he *was* of Italian descent, and I really like the name Dante. You've now probably figured out that Prosecco wasn't his last name either. However, if you must know, prosecco was for quite some time my most favorite adult beverage, and naming someone after what I consider to be the nectar of the gods is one of the highest compliments I can pay to someone. Hence, Dante Prosecco.

It was a balmy—no, make that unbearably humid—September night. My friend Marie had convinced me to go to some party (*gasp!*) off campus. As newly ordained sophomores, we still lived on campus in dorms. The majority of freshmen and sophomores did, unless they were transfer students or unlucky enough to get a bad number drawing in the lottery dorm room pickings, and then they ended up, well, *not* on campus. Back then we considered anything even two blocks off campus to be practically cross-country. Yes, we were that lazy.

But to be fair, we did feel badly for those poor souls off in no-man's-land, just not badly enough to ever really want to walk five or more minutes to drink at their places. However, there is a first for everything. Our friend Rico had a couple of unfortunate friends who lived in a huge apartment complex off campus. They were having a party, and, yes, we were invited. So was probably about every other girl those guys knew too, but that was par for the course.

As enticing as free alcohol was, I still wasn't too hip to the idea. It wasn't just the thought of walking either. It was the fact that like most off-campus abodes, the Newlands apartment complex was full of upperclassmen. Upperclassmen were scary, and I'm particularly referring to the guys, although the girls were right up there too. Upperclassmen looked you up and down or just plain stared you down when you walked into The Tavern (with your fake ID), the famed drinking establishment on campus—so much so that you'd almost do an immediate 360 and head across the street to Duke O'Neill's. At least, I usually did the 360. With the exception of a handful who were our friends, I was completely intimidated by all upperclassmen.

And I was certain that there were sure to be some at this party, since everyone was a neighbor, and a party was still a party, even if sophomores were throwing it. Over the phone, I voiced my fears to Marie. "I don't know … I mean, are we even going to know anyone at this party? And what if it's all juniors and seniors?"

"It won't be all juniors and seniors. The guys throwing it are in our class. You know Joe and Eric—they lived on the first floor last year? They're totally fun!"

"Who?" I asked. I hadn't mastered knowing everyone on campus (at least by name) like Marie had.

"*You know* Eric, who totally has a crush on you," Marie explained.

"Oh, *him*. I have no idea who you're talking about," I answered truthfully.

Whoever Eric was, I was fairly sure he absolutely did not have a crush on me. God love her, Marie was one of my biggest cheerleaders, and she was constantly telling me about all these guys who supposedly had crushes on me. Half of them I didn't even know. The way Marie talked, you'd think the whole male population at our university wanted to court me.

So, contrary to what you might think, I did not develop a super-huge head, believing everyone to worship me. I knew that Marie was prone to exaggeration (even if it was real in her mind), and I took it with a grain of salt. And I still did not want to go to this Newlands party. "Look, I don't think I want to go. You go without me," I said.

"Aw, come on. I think you should go. It'll be fun, and we might meet some new people," Marie said cheerily.

I didn't want to meet new people. Shy me? I was terrible at meeting new people. I was fine with the people we already knew and hung out with. While I loved going out, I didn't want to be in a position where

I knew no one while super-social Marie went off and chatted with everyone. I wasn't going. I answered by not answering.

Marie reasoned, "I think you should go. Besides, Rico is going, and he invited us to come."

Oh, Marie was good. She mentioned Rico, and now I *had* to go. Rico was a friend and in a bunch of classes with both of us. He was a real sweetie, an actual guy friend with no ulterior motives (i.e., he did not pretend to be our friend in hopes of getting on one of us). He was our wingman, not that we used him as such, but we always felt safe when out with him. And, no, he was not gay. But, boy, Marie was lowdown. She'd said the only possible thing that would make me feel okay to go to this party. *Rico was going.*

I sighed and said, "Fine, I'll go."

"Yay! See you in an hour," Marie shouted into the phone.

The party wasn't that bad. I do this all the time: worry, complain and bitch about things beforehand, and then end up having a grand time. It's a given. Joe and Eric were very gracious hosts. Aside from the keg on the balcony, they had an assortment of Jell-O shots and—whoa, wait for this—*food*. In college terms, Doritos and Pringles count as major food groups. And I didn't have to worry about Eric, who had a crush on me, bothering me. As I'd thought, I'd never laid eyes on him (nor him on me) before. Even better, a bunch of girls who I knew were there, and I had people to talk to while Marie and Rico went off and mingled with randoms.

Oh, and there was just a smattering of upperclassmen, but they were hanging out by the keg on the balcony. I didn't even have to get near them. I had timed it so that whenever Marie or Rico needed a beer, I did too. Then one of them would head off to the balcony, and I'd send them with my cup, as well. Yes, all in all, it was indeed shaping up to be a perfect evening.

That was until Marie went off to the balcony for another round of beers and didn't come back. At least it was taking her a lot longer than her usual five minutes. This was a problem, as I was becoming more and more parched from the double-fisted inhaling of Doritos, Pringles, and Jell-O shots in which I'd been indulging. I glanced toward the patio, trying to grab Marie's attention with my bug-eyed death stare. No such luck. She seemed enthralled with some guy she was talking to. Rico was out there, as well, but paying me no mind as he was talking to the same guy to whom Marie was talking, and he seemed mesmerized too—not in a girly way, but in a *this guy is a cool guy's guy* kind of way.

Finally, Marie looked over and caught me staring. I held up an imaginary cup and pointed to it. She smiled and jerked her head in the direction of the balcony, or actually toward the guy she was talking to, signaling me to come join them. I shook my head no. I was not a mover. Once I had my party spot, I stayed put. And my prime positioning next to the snack table, if you could call it such, made moving a definite negative. Marie nodded again. I shook my head no again. This head jerking and shaking went back and forth for another ten minutes or so. I was starting to get annoyed and also a bit worried that the girls sitting with me were beginning to think I had Tourette's syndrome or some kind of odd alcohol-induced twitch.

Marie rolled her eyes at me and came back into the room—and with no beer, I noted indignantly. She had urgent news to report from the balcony. "You need to come out *there*!" she hissed quietly while doing the head-jerking motion toward the balcony.

"Why?" I asked suspiciously, eyes narrowed.

"Because Dante wants to meet you!" Marie said imploringly.

"Who?" I asked, trying to sneak a peek (at whom, I wasn't sure) without being obvious.

Marie answered incredulously, "Dante Prosecco!"

My blank expression spurred Marie to continue hurriedly. "Dante! He's a junior, in the engineering program, a Kappa Sig. You've seen him a million times at Kappa Sig bar night …"

It was true, well, about Kappa Sigma bar night. My friends and I had frequented Kappa Sigma's Wednesday bar nights quite frequently—once a week for the past year, to be exact (excluding finals week, of course). If you must know, we had friends who belonged to the fraternity, and aside from the plethora of booze they always seemed to have, they had a variety of what we considered the cutest boys on campus—you know, in that preppy, visor-wearing way. That was the style, okay? Still, you may rest assured that I have matured somewhat, and I no longer plan my social calendar around potential booze allotment or guy (visor-wearing or not) attendance.

Again, I peeked around Marie to check out this Dante character. I had ample time to do a once-over (a few times), since he and Rico were still continuing their bromance out on the balcony. No, I'd never seen him. And I'd remember because he was really, really, I mean, *really* cute. He was tall, dark, and handsome, with short black hair, dark eyes, tanned skin, and from what I could see, a good set of teeth. I have a real thing about teeth. First, you must have some or better yet, more than just some. Second, they should be white (as opposed to gray, yellow, any variation of beige, or God forbid, brown). Third, the less snaggly, the better. In fact, don't be snaggly at all. We all have our petty pet peeves. I've become tolerant and easygoing about a lot of other things in regard to superficial looks, but not the teeth.

So, from my vantage point, Dante's teeth looked to be in quite good condition. I marveled over the fact that I had never seen him before at the Wednesday bar night or any other Kappa Sig function or even, perchance, walking to class. I'd remember a face like that. And he was wearing a very un–Kappa Sig–like getup: jeans, cowboy boots, and a white T-shirt that read "Boing! Go Bungee Jumping …" (no comment on the shirt). Who was this Dante Prosecco, and why had I never seen him?

"Who is this Dante Prosecco, and why have I never seen him?" I asked in surprise. "We *are* talking about the guy with the 'Boing!' T-shirt on, the one talking to Rico, right?" I asked Marie, lest I get my hopes up for nada.

"*Yes*, that's him." Marie smiled. "He's from Payette, on the water polo team here." I always loved how Marie had stats on everyone, my own personal background check before I even knew who the person was.

And I was intrigued by the water polo thing, since that would, of course, mean he wasn't very hairy. Well, don't they all have to shave themselves to be faster? Or is that just for speed swimming? Anyway, I mentally gave him points for probably being pretty hairless. Back then, I was by no means a connoisseur of men and had no real leg to stand on in being choosey about them, but I believe I subconsciously equated hairiness with being overly manly, and I was still a bit afraid of manly men or at least getting involved romantically with someone sporting a furry chest. Yes, kudos to Dante for being on the water polo team. Really, what else did I need to know about him?

Marie chattered away, "Anyway, he had a serious girlfriend, but she cheated on him, so he broke up with her."

"Hey, I don't wanna be some rebound girl," I said hastily. I was getting a bit ahead of myself, seeing as how I hadn't even decided if I wanted to be introduced to Dante, let alone become his rebound girl (like I even knew what a rebound girl was). However, I found myself flabbergasted at the stupidity of the girl who'd cheated on Dante. What had she been thinking?

"They dated *two years ago*, Giuliana. He's dated on and off since, nothing serious. You need to come out there. He really wants to meet you." Marie stared at me, her head tilted to one side. I looked out at the balcony, and it was then that Dante looked straight at me. I immediately looked away and felt my face flush.

I couldn't go out there. He was too cute, too good-looking to ever be interested in the likes of me. And that would become quite apparent once he actually met me.

"I can't go out there," I said in a panicky voice. "I have to go to the bathroom. My hands are … orange … from the Doritos!" I hopped up and hurried off, only to wait in line outside the bathroom with about ten other girls. By the time I made it into the bathroom, scrubbed my Dorito-y hands, and came back out, Marie was out on the balcony with Rico. And Dante was gone. I was surprised to find myself so crestfallen. I mean, I didn't even know the guy. For all I knew, maybe he was a complete loser. Why should I be upset? But I was.

I sauntered out nonchalantly and said, "Hey, so what's going on?"

Marie answered, "Well, Dante left. But …"

I waited, holding my breath.

"He wants us to stop by his apartment. He lives two doors down." *Yes! Wait, no!* Once again, the whole conflicted soul thing was setting in. What was I going to do?

Rico interjected solemnly, "He's a supercool guy, Giuliana."

"Okay," I heard myself say.

"Okay?" Rico repeated, as if checking to make sure he'd heard me correctly.

I nodded.

"We've got an affirmative. Quick, let's get her down there before she changes her mind!" Marie squealed, clapping her hands.

"Wait! What the hell am I going to say? I feel totally stupid! And you two are not allowed to leave me there alone!" I called after them. And really, I did feel totally stupid. I was no witty conversationalist around members of the opposite sex (excluding Rico and my other good guy friend, Tom). What was I going to say to Dante? *"Hi, it's so nice to meet you. I heard you dumped your cheater girlfriend. Glad to know you have a backbone. Oh, and you play water polo? That would mean you're not hairy, right?"*

"We're not going to leave you there alone. Why would we do that?" Marie rolled her eyes.

"But maybe *I* shouldn't go, though," Rico said. "I mean, he wants to meet you, Giuliana. Won't it be awkward with me, a guy, being there?"

"No, you're both going, or I don't go," I said, and I meant it. I had no courage whatsoever and was quite immature to boot. Just because I'd made out with James the year before for a fleeting moment, I had not propelled myself out of my no-gamer status. I needed my entourage of two. They'd keep me safe, and at least Marie and Rico would be able to somewhat deflect Dante's attention away from my complete dorkiness.

And that was just what happened, not that my life or young maidenhood was in any way threatened by Dante or his roommates. Apart from being introduced to each other, Dante and I hardly spoke to one another. Marie and Rico facilitated as if they were chaperoning two young Amish kids being set up for their prearranged marriage. Although a bit awkward, that was fine with me, since I'd lost all capacity to speak. To say I was tongue-tied was an understatement. I was a complete mute.

After a whopping and painful forty-five minutes, the three of us left Dante's. I felt sure he was relieved to be rid of us. Or I thought that he very well could've fancied Marie instead, what with her cuteness and the fact that she actually talked while I had more or less behaved like someone out of *Children of a Lesser God*. So I left feeling pretty much the same: lame. The endeavor had been pointless. Well, okay, I'd met Dante, and I now knew who he was and actually thought he was very cute and very nice, but I was still leaving single. So I was clearly getting ahead of myself again, wasn't I? He hadn't even asked for my number. Even I, who knew nothing, knew that if someone was interested, he'd ask for my number.

"Dante is so cool! I think he likes you!" Marie chortled as we trudged back on our journey toward the dorms. I stared at her like she had two heads before answering somewhat sarcastically, "Rigghhhtt." Marie waved me off like I was being ridiculous, but I knew she had it wrong, and I was right. Oh, when would Marie ever learn? There was absolutely no way Dante was going to ask me out.

He asked me out. I know, I was shocked too. It happened soon after at a Kappa Sig party. One of Dante's roommates approached me and pulled me aside to get the okay. "So, Dante wants to ask you out, but he's not sure if you're interested," Bobby said in a hushed tone. Yes, I know you're wondering what would have made him think that.

"Oh, no, I think he's really … uh, nice," I said truthfully. Poor choice of words, for sure, but I wasn't about to tell Bobby that I thought his roommate was a total hottie and that I was a no-dating loser who hadn't a clue how to go about these things.

Bobby was unfazed. "Cool, so he can ask for your number?"

"Um, yeah, sure," I answered with as much noncommittal coolness as I could muster. You know, it's very hard to feign easygoing nonchalance when you're secretly dying to scream, "Yes!" But that's what I did. I was a regular poker face.

"All right, I'll go tell him." It was all very junior high.

"He's coming over here!" I hissed in the direction of my friends, who began whispering excitedly. Apparently, to all, with the exception of me, Dante was well-known and quite the eligible catch on campus. I decided it was time to step up my (nonexistent) game. I was going to have to *talk* to Dante. And smile. And possibly even be funny and witty. Usually, I could pull off being *unintentionally* funny, what with my dork factor being in full effect most of the time, but to be spot-on witty was asking a lot. Fearfully, I ran off to the bathroom. I couldn't blame anything on Doritos this time, but I did actually have to go, and this would buy me some time while I organized some sort of mini monologue. *Yes, I'm auditioning for the part of someone you might possibly want to date …*

or at least ask for my phone number … or not. I trembled at the mere thought of it all. This was quite possibly going to be very awful.

When I came out of the bathroom, mentally rehearsing what I might say, Dante was standing there waiting for me.

"Hi," I said with a smile. I figured that was a good start. And then I forgot everything else I had thought to say. Rest assured, I did smile. I did speak *and* with some sort of animation. I did laugh in the appropriate places. Dante *did* laugh at some things I said. I don't remember what. In fact, I can't remember the conversational specifics at all. But he asked for my number. And I gave it to him. He called me the obligatory two days later and asked me out. I said yes to the date. He picked me up in his convertible jeep, and we went to dinner and then a movie. *I was an absolute wreck the entire time.*

It wasn't Dante, per se, who made me nervous. He was a complete gentleman and so very easygoing. In fact, he went out of his way to make me feel comfortable. It was the thought of being out on a date with someone who was obviously very smart (we didn't call engineers "enginerds" for nothing), down-to-earth, and extremely good-looking. That was a lot of pressure for a beginner's dater like myself. I mean, I might as well have been out on a date with Brad Pitt—I was that intimidated. I felt self-conscious about my awkwardness. Why couldn't I think of things to say? And what had I been thinking when I decided to wear that stupid Adrienne Vittadini knit shorts outfit? Well, I'd thought it'd been a slimming choice at the time, but everything was wrong about me. Surely Dante could see that!

He dropped me off outside my dorm. With a speedy "Thanks so much! It was a lot of fun!" I hopped out and got into the building as fast as I could. There had been no hand-holding and no good-night kiss, and I was thankful. Clearly (after my one date), I could see I was just not cut out for this dating thing. How sad that it would never work out between Dante and me. *Easy come, easy go,* I told myself, as if I was some type of high roller in the game of love.

So, we ended up dating for the entire school year. Again, I was as shocked as you are right now. I mean, who'd have thought? The relationship went like this: Dante was thoughtful and respectful of me always. I was a geeky idiot … always. Dante was constantly showering me with boyfriendy attention and in the cutest ways. On the inside I was totally elated, because I was head over heels about Dante. Do you think I'd let Dante know that, though? Of course not. I was so shy and unsure about how to act that I behaved instead as if everything was no big deal. In fact, one might think that I was actually trying to foil Dante's every attempt to woo me. I'm sure, many times, Dante did …

As was the Kappa Sig custom, boys in the fraternity sent over lowly pledges to present their girl of choice with a rose and the message that she had been invited to their formal. Somehow I'd gotten wind of what was about to happen, and I was quite worried. Why? I don't know. What was the big deal? Some guy invites you, by proxy, to a formal. It's quite a smart maneuver if you're the guy who's trying to avoid possible face-to-face rejection or if you're the girl who doesn't want to go with the particular chap. Yep, that's me, always one to look on the positive side of the spectrum.

However, for some erratic reason, I was mortified by the notion of the whole rose/invitation presentation. Yeah, count me out of *ever* being a contestant on *The Bachelor*. Most girls would've died for such gallant, if a tad mushy, pomp and ceremony. Me—I was freaked out, as usual.

Dante ever so craftily had timed it so that when he called me up (supposedly just to chat), I would be on the phone with him when the pledge showed up. As prearranged, Dante and I chatted, and soon after there was a knock on my dorm room door. I ignored it. My roommate looked at me, saw my ambivalence, and went to answer it. I shook my head furiously and waved her off. She shrugged and went back to typing on her Brother word processor. "Is someone at the door?" Dante asked.

"Um, no," I lied.

"Oh, I thought I heard a knock, "he answered.

"Nope, you're hearing things." We resumed our conversation for another ten minutes. Before getting off the phone, Dante commented, "Are you sure no one knocked at your door?"

"Yeah, no one knocked. Why?" How mean of me.

"Uh, nothing, talk to you later."

Phew! I had escaped the awkward presentation of the rose. I felt slightly terrible for having thwarted Dante's theatrical attempt at romance. At the same time, I was relieved and of course glad that he was indeed asking me to the formal. I then worried about him finding out that I had ignored the door and possibly deciding not to ask me to the formal.

A couple of hours later, Dante called me back. "Hey, I'm really sorry, but a pledge was supposed to come to your door to ask you if you'd go to the formal with me. I don't know what happened."

I did. I felt awful and ashamed for having ruined what my boyfriend thought was going to be such a sweet surprise. I was such a jerk. But better for him not to be aware of that tidbit of information for the time being or … *ever.*

"Would you go to the formal with me?" he asked.

"Yes, sure, I'd love to," I answered, and I meant it.

"Great! I still don't know how he could've missed your room," Dante said in bewilderment.

"Oh, no big deal. Probably just went to the wrong door. Don't worry about it," I answered quickly.

A month or so later, Christmas break came around. When Dante hinted about my going to Tahoe with him and his friends for New Year's Eve, I made sure to sign up to work the kids' overnighter at the local recreation department. I had worked the summer camp program there and had been hired to work the Christmas day camp anyway. So when Dante actually asked me to go up to the mountains with him, I wasn't lying about my plans.

"What? You're working? Oh, man, that's a bummer. It would've been fun. Well, that's okay," he said over the phone, and I noticed a tad disappointment.

"I know, sorry. Maybe another time for sure!" I answered. *Or the twelfth of never.*

For someone who is somewhat of an introvert and hates any type of snow sport or the vast wilderness, being stuck four or more hours away from home in the mountains with a bunch of people I didn't know sounded like a nightmare. And not only that, but how could I tell Dante that I also wasn't going because I was more than a little paranoid that perhaps he was going to expect me to finally sleep with him? Yeah, we'd yet to specifically chat about *that* topic. Tahoe (or anything else) was just not happening. I was not ready at all.

So, I had barely escaped New Year's in Tahoe, but there was no hope of escaping Valentine's Day. For weeks I obsessed about everything Valentine's-related. What kind of card would I get Dante? Something strictly funny or with a tinge of sap? I opted for funny; in fact, downright sarcasm was right up my alley. And what kind of gift would I buy for a guy I'd been going out with for five months? A framed picture of us? No, Dante had already done that for me for Christmas. Clothes? I knew a lot of girls who were giving their boyfriends cutesy Valentine's-y boxers. Uh, no. And hopefully, Dante had steered away from doing any shopping for me at Victoria's Secret. Clothing was out.

Instead, I opted for something sweet and lovable, like Dante. I picked out a cute little teddy bear, and *I made him a mixtape.* Anyone who knew me knew that if I made a mixtape, it was for someone special. Hopefully, Dante would pick up on that, since I'd been less than stellar with words. What did I put on the mixtape, you ask? Were they all romantic and cheesy songs? No, no. I put in anything I liked and/or was listening to at the time. Yes, how arrogant of me to assume that whatever I liked would be aptly cherished by the mixtape receiver. Well, it was the thought that counted anyway.

I think I put some R.E.M. on the tape. I know for sure I put Dee-Lite's "Groove Is in the Heart" on it. As a joke (kind of), I even included The Smiths' "Girlfriend in a Coma." You get it. It was just a mishmash of fun stuff. Hidden meanings of lust, etc., were not meant to be read into my song selection at all.

That's why I didn't think too much about adding another popular song of the time, The Divinyls' "I Touch Myself." I really didn't pay much attention to the lyrics; it was just a good song. Well, there was the refrain that was a little, uh, suggestive: "I don't want anybody else. When I think about you, I touch myself!" Oops. The placement of that song on the tape could *possibly* send the wrong message, I worried. Yeah, ya think? I didn't even want to think about what Dante might possibly ponder about me, or about him, or about me and him when that song came on.

However, it was too late to change the tape. I had endlessly thought it out (aside from *that* song) and slaved over making the damn tape. And I had stupidly put that song first on one side of the tape. I would have to redo that whole side, and there was no time. Well, there probably was; I was just being lazy. And anyway, I reasoned with myself, everyone was playing "I Touch Myself." *Screw it.* So there was one risqué song on the tape—big deal. Hopefully, Dante wouldn't think too much of it. Then again, I thought, maybe we should break up and thus avoid Valentine's Day and the forthcoming mixtape misunderstanding altogether.

We didn't break up. I gave Dante his teddy bear and mixtape, along with the humorous Valentine's card. He liked them all. He really did. He gave me a very cute teddy bear, almost identical to the one I gave him, except in one paw was fastened a tiny box, the kind that holds jewelry— earrings, the first jewelry I'd ever been given by a boy. I'd cherish them forever! The mother of pearl and abalone shell look just wasn't me, and I'd never wear them in a million years, but still, I'd cherish them forever.

"Wow, thank you! I love them!" I gushed self-consciously. I hadn't even gotten to the card yet either.

"Oh, just open the card later." Dante smiled.

"Oh, okay." I didn't think too much of it at the time, but the card was slightly bulky. When I opened it later, by myself, I found a deck of cards. This was odd, I thought, since I was not a cardplayer at all. And then I read the card.

"For every diamond, redeem a hug." There were a lot of diamonds. Dante had glued them back-to-back. Boy, he was crafty.

"For every heart, redeem a kiss," and there were a lot of hearts glued back-to-back, as well. Hmm, very clever. *Cute,* I thought.

"And for all the kings and queens, I'm going to leave that up to you to decide. Love, Dante." Yeah, there were a lot of kings and queens. Whoa, there it was, our sex discussion. I mean, basically, Dante was giving me the green light. The message to me signaled quite simply that he was game if I was. Was I? I didn't know. I was quite flustered. I liked Dante a lot. Sleeping with someone meant I would have to be pretty much naked, didn't it? Naked was not a good look for me. In fact, I didn't even (and still don't) enjoy parading around in a bathing suit. Okay, so I was skirting the real issue I had, which was I was just afraid and not ready. And I was embarrassed about being afraid and not ready.

We never talked about the contents of the Valentine's card. We never slept together. We broke up almost as soon as school ended. Well, when school was out, Dante and I went out to dinner once, he dropped me off at home, and then he never called me again. A week later, just knowing that something was up, I called his home and the frat house he lived in on campus, but he never returned my calls. I was devastated. Was it something I had done? Or was it something I hadn't done? Was I a boring person because I didn't sleep with Dante, or was I just a boring person period? These thoughts plagued me all summer as I cried and lamented over them to myself and to my poor friends, anyone who knew Dante, and even those who didn't—quite the same way I do to my friends now, but on a much more frantic, angst-ridden level. Nobody had an answer for me. They were all stumped too. But I knew it had to have been me. I had been true to myself, and look what had happened—I'd gotten screwed (well, actually, not screwed, but whatever).

When school started I stayed away from all Kappa Sig–affiliated parties for most of the year, lest Dante think I was trying to spy on him or ruin his game with other girls. But let's be honest, I also didn't think I could bear it if I saw him with another girl. Eventually, I heard through the school grapevine that he was dating around. I was crushed but felt it was time to move on. I guessed it'd been long enough.

I began dating a nice Theta Chi named Dan. Dan was smart and cute, and he really liked me. I thought I really liked him too. He bought me a huge fish tank with a bunch of goldfish for my birthday. It was cute, sort of, until I had to clean the algae and fish poo (do they poo?) out of the tank every other week. Mysteriously, the fish began to die off a few at a time. I swear I didn't kill them. I broke up with Dan shortly after my birthday. This was the first time I'd been the dumper in the relationship. It didn't feel good, especially when I used the awful and overused cliché of "It's really not you, it's me." Yeah, people actually do say that. But, it really was me. It had nothing to do with Dan and the stupid fish tank. I just didn't want to date anyone. I simply wasn't over Dante.

Senior year rolled around, and I vowed I would date no one that year. I didn't need it. I didn't want it. It was a hassle and could ultimately lead to no good. So what did I do? I ended up dating another Kappa Sig for the entire school year. Pat was a year younger. I remembered meeting him at a pledge party a couple of years earlier when I was dating Dante. He was adorable, with his J. Crew chino shorts, a polo, and his Jack Purcells. And I also remembered that I thought he was gay too. When

I'd mentioned that to Dante, he had laughed me off. But I knew better. My gaydar was on full alert.

That's why when Pat ended up pursuing me, I was a little taken aback. Maybe he wasn't gay. Come on, why would a gay guy pursue a girl? Of course, now I know why. But I was naive, I suppose. Back then I thought just because he was a theater major, could dress well, and was an excellent dancer didn't mean that everyone had to jump to unfair conclusions, did it? He was just misunderstood. And perhaps I was just seeing what I wanted to see. Pat was good-looking (I was attracted to him), I had someone to go to parties and formals with, and there was obviously no pressure for me to sleep with him! Yes, in the back of my mind, I totally knew he was gay. But it worked for us, at least for the school year.

During that school year, I ran into Dante at a Kappa Sig party. He had stopped by to visit the guys. We shot the breeze, and when a lull in the conversation came up, he said, "Hey, I'm really sorry for being a dick"—not exactly the words I'd been longing to hear. I was hoping for something more desperate and along the lines of "I was so wrong. Would you please take me back?" Come on, doesn't every girl fantasize about some guy who's blown her off saying that to her? No offense to Pat, but I would've straightaway thrown him under the bus (or into the makeshift mosh pit going on in the middle of the room) and jumped into Dante's arms that instant. I think Pat would've been okay with that too. Pat, if you ever read this, you know I absolutely love you.

Anyway, it was too late for Dante and me to go back. I accepted his apology and said I was sorry too. I'll never know for sure why it ended, although, as I've said, I have my speculations. But I was truly sorry for Dante feeling that maybe I had never really liked him. It's been twenty years, and Dante still retains his legendary status among my friends. "God, he was gorgeous!" "He was *so* nice!" "Remember when he barbecued for all of us when we got home from the bar at 2:00 a.m.?"

And me? You needn't worry that I've been carrying a torch for Dante all these years. I've seen him a couple of times at friends' parties and have even met his wife. It's been wonderful to see him and catch up. No, I'm not in love with him. Was I in love with him in college? Being young and immature, I don't know if I even knew what love was then.

However, he'll always hold a very special place in my heart—not only for barbecuing for me and my tipsy friends at two in the morning but for being the all-around good guy who liked—no, actually adored—me and even acted like so. So even if he "was a dick" (his words) who slightly fractured my heart, cheers to Mr. Dante Prosecco.

"You're So Vain. You Probably Think This Chapter's about You ..."

I won't put you to sleep by delving into the rest of my twenties. It was a weird and uncertain sort of limbo, graduating from college and trying to find a career for myself. And basically, my dating life back then would bore you to tears. While I kissed some boys and dated a bit (never anyone for more than a month or so at a time), aside from the blunder years of college, it was a big snoozer of a decade. Fast-forward to the beginning of my thirties, and (among others) enter the Irish.

I can safely say that my infatuation with the Irish started way back in grammar school. My mother, being a teacher and having a plethora of papers to correct and meetings to attend after school, and wanting to give my grandparents a break, would frequently send my sister and me to an Irish woman named Bridie Mahoney. Bridie had children who went to school with us, and she babysat a gaggle of kids, infants to school age. I never minded going to Bridie's house. I loved the Waterford crystal and shamrock-laden Belleek trinkets scattered about the house. Bridie was funny, and I was mesmerized by her Irish accent. And she always called us "Pet." "Come here, Pet. Will you have a snack? Oh, you will, you will. Good girl, yourself." And it was at Bridie's that I was first introduced to Neil Diamond. How could I not have fond memories? To this day, whenever I hear "Shilo," I'm transported back in time to Bridie's playroom, where a bunch of us kids would sit around the record player and listen to Bridie's Neil Diamond album. *Good times.*

Going to Bridie's made me want to be Irish or, at least, more Irish than I was. Mostly Italian, with some Danish and Portuguese, I was only a bit Irish. So, of course, I was always intrigued by the stories my Italian noni would tell me of my great-great-great-grandparents, Sarah and Jack Hughes, from Cork, who settled in California and owned, of all things (note sarcasm here), a saloon. The whole saloon thing would explain a lot about me. Anyway, suffice it to say, the little amount of Irish I had in me just didn't seem enough. Unfortunately, there's not much you can do about your ancestry.

However, you never know who you're going to end up making friends with. Josie was from County Tipperary and taught with my mom. Only a couple of years younger than me, she and I hit it off, and when she and her Irish fiancé decided to go back to Ireland to wed, she extended the invitation to my mom, my sister, and me.

"Now, don't worry if you can't go. Plane tickets are very dear, and I will totally understand," Josie would insist.

She needn't have worried. Oh, I was going. The thought of not going had never entered my mind. Finally, here was the chance to go to Ireland, the Emerald Isle, the land of meat and potatoes, of Guinness, and of people who had, yes, Irish accents. I wasn't a Guinness drinker, but all the rest sounded fabulous to me. And maybe I'd meet a cute Irish guy who sang like Bono and looked like Colin Farrell. God knows I wasn't meeting anyone at home. Ireland it was!

My sister and I hit Ireland, and it was everything I'd imagined it to be times infinity. Fifty shades of green and any other cliché you've heard, Ireland was. And I loved it all. And the guys were gorgeous. Maybe I just get overtaken by an accent, but I was quite smitten. On our way to visit the Cliffs of Moher, we stopped in Ballyvaughan to do a little shopping and, as girls typically do, look for a restroom. Walking down the street, a gentleman called to me, "Ye must be from California."

I stopped in my tracks and said, "Why, yes, I am." I'm no double for anyone in the cast of *Baywatch*, so who was this soothsayer? What could have given my homeland away?

He smiled and, with a twinkle in his eye, said, "All the best-lookin' ones are. Good day," and walked off. *I knew I liked this country,* I thought as I shouted a "Thank you!" after him. Of course, he was about sixty, was missing a few teeth, and had a dirty Irish-knit fishing cap on, but a compliment was a compliment. I was charmed for sure.

Alas though, aside from my toothless admirer in Ballyvaughan,

I met no other men of the Irish species. It was quite disappointing. The closest I got to kissing anything at all was when we visited the Blarney Stone. And then I was made to do it twice, since according to the eighty-plus-year-old man holding me upside down, I'd missed it the first time. Yeah, that'll happen when you're not only hungover, but afraid of heights, so you have your eyes closed while you're suspended head down over a huge rock that you hope you aren't dropped on. Go figure.

Since that first trip to Ireland, I've been back four more times, and every time for a wedding. I've still never met anyone. In fact, I've met more Irish folks at home than in Ireland. That said, it was quite ironic that a month after I'd gotten home from Josie's wedding I met Seamus.

Just back from her honeymoon, Josie called me up and invited me to a party at Mullan's Bar, another local Irish establishment. Her sister-in-law was turning thirty, and the party was going to be huge. And there would be a DJ. *Irish people, in an Irish bar, and a DJ?* Like I needed any more convincing. Still, I was a tad worried that I wouldn't know anyone except Josie, and I didn't want to completely hover around her all night if she wanted to mingle with family and friends.

"Are you sure it's all right? I don't want to be a party crasher," I told her.

"Oh, sure, it'll be fine. The restaurant and bar will still be open to everyone, so there'll be *loads* of other people there. And you'll know people from the wedding. But feel free to bring some friends!"

I roped my good friend Jane into going. She even offered to drive. I was a bit nervous showing up. I dreaded the whole opening of the bar door, where everyone turns around and gives you the eye, wondering, *Who are the Yanks?* It's true, it happens. Luckily for us, the party was in full session. Not much notice was given to us. A silver-haired seventy-five-year-old Irish guy was serenading the crowd while people of all ages danced around the makeshift dance floor. As soon as he was done, the DJ started up with the likes of Gloria Gaynor's "I Will Survive." It was a party all right.

We sat with Josie, drank our drinks, and people watched. In true Irish form, Josie filled us in about the partygoers. "See your man over there? Well ..." As they say, it was great *craic* (pronounced *crack*, meaning a plain old good time and not to be confused with the hardcore drug supposedly not favored by Whitney Houston). While Josie introduced us to many people, we met no one. No one wanted to chat with us. No one stopped by to introduce themselves. I thought it was odd, but we were at someone's party where everyone already knew each other. Why would they bother with us?

And then *he* walked by. There were a few tables of people between us, and I'm not quite sure why I happened to look over at that exact moment, but I did. I wouldn't have taken much notice except that he was staring at me as he passed by. He caught me watching him watching me, and I quickly looked away. *Great,* I thought, *now he probably thinks I'm playing the coy card,* when in actuality, he'd probably been staring at someone else or possibly the hanging lantern above my head. *Too bad, he seemed kind of cute,* in the two seconds I'd laid eyes upon him. I put the thought out of my mind, since a ton of people had been staring at us anyway, wondering who the non-Irish party crashers were.

Midnight was fast approaching. That's how much fun we were having even just sitting and chatting to ourselves. I mean, for goodness sakes, I felt like I was back in Ireland on vacation again. As usual, I could've stayed to the very end, but Jane was getting a little antsy, and I couldn't blame her, since she was the designated driver and not able to fully participate in the Irish reveling going on around us. And that was when *he* sat down at our table.

"Hello," he said, looking directly at me. He was Irish, but I couldn't help but think his hello came out sounding like Anthony Hopkins from *The Silence of the Lambs.* We all remember "Hello, Clarice," don't we? Despite the cocktails I'd imbibed, I was still wary. Who was this Irish guy, (inadvertently) impersonating Anthony Hopkins, who actually wanted to sit down and chat?

"Hello," I answered with one raised eyebrow. I waited with baited breath, hoping whatever came out of his mouth next didn't involve eating a census taker's liver with some fava beans and a nice Chianti.

I was in luck. "Do you have a name?" he asked with twinkling eyes. I wasn't sure if the twinkling eyes were actually glassy from drinking, but to the naked eye he appeared to be sober.

"Giuliana," I said and then added quickly, "and these are my friends, Jane and Josie."

"Hello." He nodded at both of the girls and then said, "I'm Seamus."

"Nice to meet you," I answered.

"What's your last name, Seamus?" Josie asked, as would any Irish person worth their salt. It was a question I'd been wondering myself. While I'm all about the accent, I love a good Irish name too.

"McVane," he said. *Hmm, I've never heard that one before,* I thought, as if I was some genealogical expert on Irish surnames.

"Whereabouts are you from? Are you from up north?" Josie continued her heritage check. I was quite enjoying this, as I didn't have to say a thing while still gathering necessary information.

"Yes, from Tyrone," Seamus answered.

Josie continued, "Ah, I thought so. I think I've seen you at the gym before. Do you go to Prime Athletic?" And indeed, Seamus and Josie did frequent the same gym. In fact, this was the very gym I also went to. Funny, I'd never seen him around.

"Here, let me get you ladies a round of drinks," he said, and before we could protest (not that we would have), he wandered off to the bar.

Josie hit me in the arm. "He's not bad, Giuliana! He's got his eye on you. I don't know much about him, but, oh, he drives a *lovely* silver Mercedes. I've seen him getting out of it at the gym."

I'm not a fan of guys in sports cars—too showy for me. But if the Mercedes meant this guy actually worked and had a decent-paying job, I wasn't completely opposed. And who was I to judge, as I was still driving the Honda Civic (with no air conditioning) that I'd bought straight out of college? I shrugged. I had yet to reach a conclusion about Seamus, but he was up a point for buying my friends and me a round of drinks. He returned with our drinks (and nothing for himself, I noted), which put a stop to any conversation we'd been having about him.

And then the small talk began, and this time, unfortunately, it involved me. It had only been a matter of time. What did I do for a living? I explained I was a teacher at a Catholic school. I found out Seamus was a carpenter. *At least he can fix things,* I thought. I can't stand guys who don't know how to fix things. I'm the worst. I was not blessed with the ability to follow DVR or any or other appliance-type directions. I can change lightbulbs, and that's about it, and to be honest, I really don't care. However, I find it irritating and just totally unmanly if a guy can't fix things. So, score another point for Seamus. And he was actually good-looking, with short blondish hair, bright green eyes, and good teeth. I tried to inconspicuously scrutinize his outfit, which was an orange short-sleeved linen button-up, jeans, and flip-flops. *Not bad.*

The DJ began blasting Will Smith's "Gettin' Jiggy Wit It," and Jane yelled, "Ooh, let's go dance!"

Jane, Josie, and Seamus all stood up. I waved them off. "You guys go. I'll stay here." Remember, I'm not a mover. I didn't want to get jiggy, even if everyone else in the place was. Josie and Jane headed toward the dance floor. Seamus stood there staring at me. "Go ahead, go ahead, dance with the girls," I said hastily as I took a sip of my drink.

"Come on," he said, and before I knew what was happening, he'd grabbed my hand and was dragging me toward the dance floor. I was not happy.

It was open season on the dance floor. Everyone was out there. There were eighty-year-olds twirling each other around, there were fake IDers hip-hopping, and there was the birthday girl and all her friends. And a party's not a party without someone sporting a blonde Viking wig with braids, now, is it? Oddly enough, the Viking wig was making its way around the dance floor. One minute it'd be on someone's head, and then just as suddenly someone else would drunkenly yank it off the person's head and put it on. It was quite entertaining. However, I didn't want that thing touching my head. In fact, I would have preferred to be back at my table, enjoying the dance floor shenanigans from afar.

Guess who got in on the wig action. No, not me, but Seamus, who had all of a sudden become a complete dancing fool. Not only did he capture and secure the Viking wig, but he picked up Josie and practically held her over his head (à la *Dancing With the Stars*) and spun around. It was impressive because Josie was a foot taller than Seamus and also because it wasn't me. I hoped Josie didn't toss her Coors Light. While everyone clapped and continued their jigginess, I watched in horror as Seamus set a somewhat dizzy and now staggering Josie down, then grabbed Jane, and did the same. I had reason to believe and fear that I would be next. Abhorring any type of unwanted attention and having a very short skirt on, I understood my cue to bolt from the dance floor.

I returned to the safety of our table, and luckily my drink was still there. I wondered if Seamus was drunk. He didn't seem drunk, but who could—who *would*—dance like that without being under the influence? I berated myself at once. Not *everyone* had to drink to have a good time. I wasn't one of them, but, hey, maybe Seamus was, or else he was just a complete extrovert/attention whore.

A song or two later, the girls, along with a bewigged Seamus, came back to the table. Plunking himself down next to me, Seamus looked at me and said, "So, can I get your number? Maybe we can go to the city sometime, go to dinner and out dancing." If this was any indication of how he normally behaved on a dance floor, I was going to have to decline.

"Um, how about coffee instead? I mean, we barely know each other. For all I know, you could be an axe murderer," I joked ... kind of.

With a smirk, he answered, "Now do I look like an axe murderer?"

No, but then again, nobody thought Ted Bundy looked spooky either. I wondered if Ted Bundy had ever donned a wig. While I wavered, Jane spoke up. "Well, I have a few questions before you get my friend's number."

Seamus nodded, and Jane continued, "Do you have any tattoos?" Uh, I wasn't sure where Jane was going with this. Who really cared if he had a tattoo, as long as it wasn't a swastika, a naked lady, or 666?

"No," Seamus answered.

"All right," Jane said. "Have you ever been in jail?" Okay, I breathed a sigh of relief. Jane was back on track with her inquisition. It was a sound question indeed, and one that I usually forgot to ask.

"No," said Seamus.

"Good," replied Jane. "And one more ..."

I was expecting something like "How old are you?" or "Ever been married before?" or even perhaps "Boxers or briefs?"

Instead, Jane asked, "Are you in the IRA?"

"*Jane!*" I shouted in mortification. "Not everyone from Northern Ireland is in the IRA!" Of course, with my luck, surely, a (possible) terrorist in a wig would totally be interested in asking me out.

Jane looked at me and said with a smile, "It's a valid question, Giuliana." Josie laughed as I rolled my eyes in embarrassment.

Seamus said earnestly, "No, I'm not in the IRA, and I have no political opinions whatsoever."

"Well then, it's fine with me if you get Giuliana's number!" Jane said brightly. "Sorry though, Seamus, but we're gonna have to take off, since I'm the driver tonight."

"So, can I get your number?" he asked again.

I am against giving out my number in bars. I really am. It's so cheesy. But at least Josie, if she didn't exactly know Seamus, knew of him and could easily ask around the local Irish grapevine. Seamus wasn't a complete stranger.

"Only if you take off that wig," I said.

"Done," he said and jerked the wig off his head. I gave him my number, and Jane and I hugged Josie good-bye and left. Getting into Jane's car, she commented, "Well, he seems nice, but an Irishman with no political opinions? That seems a bit odd to me."

I had no idea, but I wasn't going to worry about it unless he actually called me and asked me out.

A couple of days later, I answered my cell phone. It was Seamus.

"Hello, dear. How are you?" he asked. Was it too soon for him to be calling me "dear"? I wondered. Normally, I would've said yes, but I had to admit that being said with an Irish accent actually made it quite cute. For all I knew, maybe he called everyone "dear," but it was fine with me. For once, I wasn't put off by a guy's (albeit harmless) presumptuousness. How unusual.

We talked about the weather and what we were up to that fine Labor Day, and he finally asked, "So where is it you live?"

I took a breath before answering. This was a question I dreaded, especially when it came from some guy who might be romantically interested. I still lived at home with my mother. I know, I know, you don't have to tell me ... I was thirty and still at home. *Lame.* Must I remind you of my late-bloomer issues? Unlike a lot of peers my age, I just didn't have a problem with it most of the time, except when meeting guys. Yeah, and the guys definitely seemed to have a problem with it.

Upon hearing I lived at home, most boys made a speedy exit. It was a given. "Oh ... well, it was really nice meeting you. Catch up with you, uh, some other time," they'd say as they backed away, knocking down lamps, people, bar stools, you name it. As they did so, I could pretty much read their minds. "Black Hawk down! She lives at home! There'll be no sleepovers with that one. Abort mission immediately!"

Yes, I was quite accustomed to that typical male response. However, I had finally decided to take the plunge and move. Marie was looking for a roomie and had convinced me I was it. So within weeks, I'd be moving to, wait, not the chic urban likes of San Francisco, but to … well, a nice little suburb about fifteen minutes from where I grew up. Please, baby steps, people.

So, I actually had a decent response to Seamus's question but would still have to mention I was living at home. *Ugh.*

"Well, I'm living at home right now, but I'm moving at the end of the month to Parkside." I waited for the click and dial tone in my ear.

"I can't believe it," Seamus said in shock. Yep, here it came. I supposed he couldn't believe what a loser I was.

"I just can't believe it. I just met you, and now you're moving away from me!" he said in disappointed disbelief. I was speechless.

He continued seriously, "Could you not just stay at your mother's? Why would you want to pay rent?" I didn't. In fact, I'd been avoiding it for years but had somehow thought it was time to put on my big girl pants and act like an actual grown-up. Believe me, I didn't want to. Needless to say, I was now the one in disbelief. I mean, he hadn't feigned that his phone was on the fritz and hung up on me already, per the usual. Seamus didn't care if I lived at home. I knew it was a little early in the game, but was it possible I'd hit the jackpot?

I didn't have much time to ponder that question, since Seamus asked, "Well, would you like to go to dinner sometime this week?" Yes, I did. We settled on a day and a time and hung up. I had a date with an Irish boy. Color me excited!

A few evenings later, I waited a bit nervously in the kitchen for Seamus to arrive. What if I couldn't understand anything he said? I'd had to ask him to repeat quite a few times on the phone because of his accent. Hopefully I'd be more successful reading lips. I fretted. What if this turned out to be a bust? What if he really wasn't cute? I mean, perhaps I'd just been lured in by the Irish accent. *He was cute, right?* I asked myself worriedly, but Seamus in a mangy Viking wig was the only vision that kept popping into my head. Well, if nothing else, at least I'd get to ride in the "lovely" silver Mercedes Josie had gone on about.

As I thought of how I could exit the house when Seamus arrived without alerting my mother and sister (who still lived at home too), my mom spoke up from the TV room. "Have him come in. I want to meet him."

I wasn't sure if I wanted her meeting Seamus. Well, it wasn't so much the meeting part; it was the twenty questions part.

"Fine, but don't ask him too many questions, okay?" I said.

My mother rolled her eyes. "I'm not going to ask too many questions, but I want to meet him." She wasn't fooling me. Of course, my mother was going to ask him questions. It was her job. In fact, we all know *The Handbook for Mothers* commands one to do so. However, this mostly occurs during one's teen years. Ah, the joys of living at home when you're *thirty*. So much for sneaking out.

"I'm not in high school," I mumbled irritably under my breath.

"What's that?" my mom called from across the room. All of a sudden the woman had bionic hearing.

"Nothing," I muttered. A car horn honked outside. He was here! The garage door was open, and I peeked out the door. There he was, sitting in his lovely silver Mercedes and thankfully without a Viking wig on. I waited for him to turn off the engine and get out of the car. He sat there, in his car, engine running. He showed no sign of turning it off or getting out either.

"Is he honking his horn at you? He needs to come in. You don't come out for someone who honks his horn on a first date," my mom said pointedly as she got up from her chair, ready for her inquisition.

I hated to admit it, but I agreed with my mother. *What the hell?* This wasn't the Indy 500. I mean, if he didn't even stop the car for me to get in, was he going to expect me to jump out and roll to a stop as he did a drive-by at the end of the date? Who did he think he was? Who did he think I was? I was huffy already, and the date hadn't even started. Not good.

I sauntered out and waved to him to come inside. He saw me, and I turned and walked back in without waiting for him. If he didn't like that, he could drive on. I hoped he didn't, though. How mortifying. A few moments later, Seamus stepped into the kitchen.

"Hello," he said with a smile as he glanced from me to my mother.

"Hi," I said. *Good, he's still cute.* "Seamus, this is my mom. Mom, this is Seamus." While the How-do-you-dos were going on, I called over my shoulder, "I'll be right back. I'm gonna grab a jacket and my purse."

Seamus could fend for himself. Besides, my mother wasn't very scary. I came back and waited while my mother laughed her signature laugh at whatever Seamus had been saying. "Ah, ha-ha, ha-ha!" Apparently, I needn't have worried about leaving the two of them together. Seamus seemed just fine. I think I was annoyed by that. The guy should at least be just a little bit nervous. My mother really needed to work on her parental scare tactics, I thought.

"Ready?" Seamus turned to me.

"Sure," I said.

"It was nice to meet you." Seamus smiled at my mom.

"Nice to meet you too. Have a good time!" my mom called as we went out through the garage. As we walked down the driveway, it was then that I realized Seamus had left the motor of his car running. I was taken aback. I didn't know anything about Irish boys. Was this something they normally did—leave a car running, unattended? Not only was I taken aback, but I was slightly offended. Was I not worth an engine turnoff?

"Do you always leave your car running when you're not in it?" I asked bluntly.

"Sometimes," he answered with a smile. I raised my eyebrows.

"Sorry, was I supposed to turn it off?" he asked sheepishly.

"Well, most people do ... turn off their cars ... when they get out of them for anything longer than ... two seconds," I replied sarcastically.

"Ah, well, next time I'll make sure to turn it off." He smiled. I didn't know if there was going to be a next time. I was annoyed. I wanted the date to be over with. Too bad he was cute and Irish.

We had dinner at an "Italian" restaurant. It was what I like to snobbishly refer to as a "fake Italian" restaurant (i.e., they serve soft bread sticks, they don't serve prosecco, tiramisu is their only dessert, and they pronounce bruschetta "bru-SHETTA"). No, it wasn't the Olive

Garden (since there were no all-you-can-eat garlic bread sticks or pasta dishes). It was a chain restaurant a slight step above. I decided not to be too harsh, since Seamus was foreign and perhaps he thought this was legit Italian fare. What did I care? It was a free dinner.

Not that I ate anything. This was when I used to not eat on dates. I'm not sure why. I was about twenty pounds thinner than I am now. I needed to eat. Now, I don't care so much. Bring on the food, and, yes, I'll probably even have some (*gasp!*) bread from the bread basket too. I may still be quite vain about my looks, but I am also hungry. And I find vanity tends to go out the window on an empty stomach.

As I was saying, I didn't eat much. Seamus and I shared bruschetta, which our waiter completely butchered in pronunciation, Seamus had some kind of messy lasagna, and I had a Caesar salad and a Diet Coke. *Boring* (the food was). The conversation and company, on the other hand, were pretty good. In fact, they were better than good. I was having fun in spite of my previously huffy mood. I was surprised, what with the whole off-putting running-car thing.

I found Seamus interesting. He was one of five children, the second born. He'd come out to Chicago a few years earlier to play Gaelic football and, as many of the Irish do, ended up staying longer and eventually moved out to San Francisco. Apparently, there was not a lot going on in Tyrone, work-wise, and a better living could be made out here.

I am fascinated by individuals who have the guts to leave everything they know to go to another country and not, like myself, just for a vacation. Here I was still living at home at thirty! It was a reality check for sure. While I was embarrassed by my babyish lack of gumption, I was impressed and humbled by Seamus and his work ethic. And he called home once a week to talk to his mother. I liked that. I did. Coming from a single-parent home, with one sister, our extended family didn't include much more than just my paternal noni and my maternal grandparents. That said, we were close, since we were all we had. Perhaps that's why I'd stuck around home for so long. Believe me, I wanted to be "free," but there was a certain comfort in needing my family and in being needed. I mattered, even if I was just taking out the garbage once a week.

Suffice it to say, I liked that Seamus seemed to adore his mother. On a somewhat subconscious level, I was on the lookout for someone who'd understand and support my strong familial ties. He was fitting the bill quite nicely. With dinner over, Seamus drove me home. He pulled up in front of the house, and while he didn't turn the ignition off, he did stop the car, so thankfully there was no need for a stunt double.

"Well, thank you. It was fun," I said, opening the car door. On a first date, I do not like to awkwardly linger while exiting the car. No, sir, I am all business. Get that door open and one foot out as soon as possible to avoid a kiss (if you don't like him) or the painful silence (if he doesn't like you). If, perchance, he does like you, well, your speediness will probably baffle him, and he won't know what to think, but at least you won't have made a fool of yourself. At least, that's what I thought.

"All right, dear, I'll call you later." He smiled.

"Okay, talk to you later!" I closed the car door behind me.

I'd made it through the dreaded first date. And I didn't hate Seamus. He didn't hate me either. In fact, he appeared to find me quite interesting and entertaining, a promising start. It was official: I liked Seamus.

Things progressed well, like they should, when two people actually like each other. However, I was (pleasantly) surprised by Seamus's constant and, shall I say, overly enthusiastic effort. And before you go thinking I'm just being my negative, deprecating self again, let me explain.

We were only two weeks into knowing each other and had been out a couple of times. I answered my phone on a Sunday afternoon, and it was Seamus. Wow, I'd just seen him Friday night, and here he was calling me way before the leave-it-till-Wednesday- night-to-call phone call. My stomach jumped in anticipatory glee.

"So, what are you up to today?" he asked a few minutes into our conversation.

"I'm at my grandma's house. My mom and sister and I are over for dinner." My grandfather had passed away a few years earlier, and it had since become a family tradition for the three of us to go to Grandma's on Sunday afternoons and stay for dinner. I figured if Seamus was okay with my living with my mom, I might as well throw in Sundays with Grandma too and get that out of the way. It was just what we did. Before he could say anything, I added, "What are you up to?"

"Oh, nothing. Nothing," Seamus answered, and I noted what

sounded like wistfulness. I could've sworn I heard a sigh somewhere in there too. Was he hinting that he wanted to come over to Grandma's? No guy in his right mind would want to meet the family so soon in the wooing process. The likelihood of him coming to Grandma's, should I invite him, was slim to none. Therefore, I decided to be polite and just ask. I was fully prepared for him to suddenly remember some plans that he'd forgotten he had.

"Well, you're welcome to come over if you feel like it," I said nonchalantly.

Before I knew it, Seamus said, "Sure, I'd love to. Where does your grandmother live?"

Huh? "Uh, she, uh, lives, uh …" I was flustered as I gave him the address. If he noticed the complete befuddlement in my voice, he didn't let on.

"Great, I'll see you in a bit," he said and hung up.

Shit, Seamus is coming to dinner. I could hardly believe it. Why was he coming to dinner? This was not normal guy protocol. What was the matter with him? He had no plans at all? *Really?* Or was he lonely and missing being around his family? Or did he just really want to see me? If the latter was so, I was going to have to ditch him pretty quickly. I mean, who would like me that much so soon? It just didn't happen in my world. Generally speaking, I was used to admiring from afar, very afar, or simply having the objects of my attraction run the other way before they even knew I was actually attracted to them. So, this was new. I really had no clue as to what to do in this type of scenario.

I quickly came to my senses and decided first things first. I was going to have to break the news to the ladies that we would be having a dinner guest. This would be less than fun (for me). Mom would excitedly start making up her list of questions to ask Seamus, which would surely include asking about what particular parish his family belonged to, as if she'd actually known anyone in that particular parish in County Tyrone, Northern Ireland. Somehow she'd also finagle out of him whether he was a Catholic or a Protestant, and if Catholic, what was his confirmation name? I wondered if she could work in asking how old he was. He looked to be about my age, but I hated to be too nosy. I'd leave that to my mom.

Grandma, on the other hand, who (much to our chagrin) still insisted on cooking, would have a fit about Seamus coming over, since this evening's menu consisted of plain old pot roast and spaghetti. I could hear her ranting already. *Oh, Giuliana, why couldn't you have told me sooner? I could've gotten a leg of lamb at least!* After she got over her initial freak-out, she'd then become ecstatic at the possibility of my future husband coming to dinner. She was utterly concerned and shocked that I was as old as I was and not only not married, but habitually single. I would remind her that she was twenty-six when she got married, which was *ancient* in her time, but that would fall on deaf ears (literally). I then shuddered thinking about what typical comments she might utter once she'd had a few glasses of wine.

"I promised my husband I wouldn't die until Giuliana got married. But, God, I'm so tired of living! She's taking too long! So glad you could come to dinner, Shamoo."

Grandma was famous for annihilating the English language. If I had a dollar for every time I heard her say "Domino Placebo" for Plácido Domingo, there'd be no need for me to work anymore. She was sure to mispronounce Seamus's name. And after the name debacle, she'd offer some dessert, her favorite, Viennetta ice cream, which she still called Vendetta. "Would you like some Vendetta, Shamoo?" We'd given up correcting Grandma's misnomers years ago. In fact, we found them quite humorous, but, oh, I was cringing in embarrassment already.

And let's not forget about my younger sister. Annie wouldn't say much. In fact, she'd barely talk to Seamus at all, but she'd scrutinize him with intimidating stares the whole night. Once he left, she'd say smugly, "I don't like him. I get a bad vibe off him. I get vibes, you know." Yes, I knew. She got bad vibes about everyone. Shockingly, she was still single too.

The writing was on the wall. After tonight's dinner, there was no way Seamus would be interested in sticking around. On the upside, Grandma would still be alive, and, to her dismay, for quite some time her dreams of marrying me off would be trampled once again. I thought about calling Seamus and warning him about what he was about to encounter. Nah, why bother? I'd let the chips fall where they may. If he couldn't handle the family, well, there was no point in bothering, and I might as well find out sooner rather than later.

An hour later, a knock sounded at the back kitchen door. There was Seamus peeking in the window. While I wondered why he'd chosen the back door instead of ringing the doorbell at the front door, Grandma shouted hysterically, "Oh, God! Why is he at the back door? I don't want people coming in through the *kitchen!*"

It was as if we were the Rockefellers and Seamus was committing the gravest of faux pas by entering through the service entrance. I shrugged. "I don't know." Grandma shook her head, sighed, and then threw her head in her hands, as if this was the worst thing to happen since Vatican II. You may have sensed this is most likely from where I get my dramatic flair.

My mom shushed Grandma. "*Mom,* calm down, would you?"

"Don't tell me to calm down! I don't want guests coming in through the kitchen!" Grandma shouted from behind her hands.

Mom rolled her eyes. My sister laughed and mumbled, "Ha-ha. Oh, boy, here we go."

I shot them all my dirtiest look (the one that I normally use on my students) and swatted my hand at them, hissing, "All of you, *be quiet!*"

"What did she say?" Grandma yelled, tapping her hearing aids in annoyance.

"Nothing!" both my mom and sister answered.

"Well, you don't have to yell at me! Oh, these damn hearing aids!" Grandma shrieked back.

"Oh, God, help me," I muttered under my breath and then opened the door with a smile. "Hello!"

The dinner was a success. Grandma's top-of-the-line yet nonetheless problematic hearing aids magically worked that evening. For the most part, she could hear everything, and Seamus's name was safe from excessive butchering. If I didn't know better, I would swear my grandmother was flirting with him. She absolutely fawned over him, quite like she does over her priest friends when they come to dinner. And miraculously, Grandma refrained from making her favorite comment of wanting me to get married so she could finally die.

Seamus good-naturedly indulged my mother with her myriad

of questions. By the end of dinner I knew the names and ages of his siblings, his birthday, how tall he was, and his mother's maiden name. I was impressed. My mother really should've pursued a career with the FBI or at least become a private investigator. Although she hadn't unearthed Seamus's age, the one thing I was now dying to know and the only thing I really wanted to know at this point, I had to admit her questioning skills were off the hook.

Even my sister was on good behavior. She kept her skeptical glares to a minimum and even talked to Seamus. Yes, everyone was cooperating. Of course, I'd wait and hear what they really thought once Seamus left. Seamus left with a doggie bag of pot roast and a hug from Grandma. "You come back anytime for dinner, but make sure you come to the front door!"

He said he'd call me later.

I closed the door behind him and looked at the three ladies.

"Well, he's a very nice boy. I couldn't understand half of what he said, but he seems very nice!" Grandma said enthusiastically and went off into the kitchen. Of course, while I wanted Grandma to like Seamus, I wasn't too worried about her opinion, since he could've had a third eye, and she wouldn't have cared. A heartbeat and the fact that a male was coming to dinner were usually the only necessary credentials in which she was interested. What I really wanted to know was what my mom and sister thought.

"Well?" I said, looking at the two of them.

My mom smiled and said, "He's very nice."

"Do you think he's cute?" I asked pointedly. I don't know why it mattered, since I already thought he was cute.

"Yes, he's handsome," my mom answered assuredly.

I turned to look at my sister. "So?"

Annie shrugged. "He seems nice."

"You hate him," I said.

Annie rolled her eyes. "I *just* met him. He seems nice enough, but let's just say the jury's still out on him." Coming from my sister, I guessed that was good enough. At least she hadn't talked about her vibes.

"But, *Mom*, you were supposed to find out how old he was," I said in exasperation.

"I did. You were in the kitchen doing the dishes."

"What?" I nearly screamed. Boy, my mother was good.

"Yeah," my sister added, "he's twenty-five."

My face literally fell. *Twenty-five? Oh, no.* He was … young. I was … old. Well, thirty compared to twenty-five seemed Jurassic to me back then. Now, I'd give anything to be thirty—or not even to be thirty, but I'd consider dating someone a mere five years younger to actually be ideal. But back to my cradle-robbing dilemma …

Oh, this was just awful. I couldn't date Seamus. He was too young! I should've known there'd be something wrong with him.

"What's the matter?" my mom asked.

"He's twenty-five!" I shouted.

"I knew she was going to have a fit about it," Annie stated.

"Well, wouldn't you? I can't date him. He's too young! Don't you think?" I looked at my mom and sister skeptically.

My mom rolled her eyes. "Giuliana, I really don't think it matters. He seems pretty mature. He's been on his own, working, for over four years."

Yeah, sure, but back to me. Did he know how old I was? What twenty-five-year-old would want to date a thirty-year-old?

Annie interjected, "Whatever. Anyway, he looks *way* older than you. He totally has crow's-feet. Didn't you see them?"

Jeez, my sister was so critical. However, yes, I had seen them. Ah, my sister knew me well. She was appealing to my very, *very* vain side. While I felt that the five-year age difference was enormous, I was more concerned with not wanting to *look* like I was thirty. *If Seamus is only twenty-five, fine, as long as he looks my age or older.* However, I was still on the fence about this. The thought of people judging my age and thinking me to be a bit long in the tooth was frightful. Oh, those were the days.

"So, what are you going to do?" my sister asked.

"I don't know," I said gloomily.

What *was* I going to do? I did know. I was just going to have to bring up the whole age topic and then end it with Seamus, and preferably before he found out my age and went MIA of his own accord. Once again, I was quite disappointed in how short-lived Seamus's and my

May/December romance was going to become. Well, that was the way it had to be. I just did not date younger men. I disqualified my old college beau, Patrick, since he'd only been a year younger and … gay. Yes, his gaiety totally nixed him.

When Seamus called the next night, I was ready but not completely willing. I really didn't want to have the age conversation. I wished it wasn't an issue. I felt let down again. Why was I so unlucky in love? Why were the odds always stacked against me?

"So, what are your plans for this Friday night? Do you want to go to dinner or something?" Wow, this had to be a record. A guy was asking me out on a Monday for a Friday. Typical, now that I was no longer going to be able to date him since I was *old*.

"Nothing, but, well, uh … I didn't know you were twenty-five," I said quite lamely.

"I am. Why? How old are you?" he answered.

Oh, boy, here it came.

"Thirty," I said, trying not to sound like it was the death sentence I felt it to be.

"Oh. Well, does it bother you that you're thirty or that I'm twenty-five?" Seamus asked, and he didn't seem the least bit put off.

"Both," I answered truthfully and then chuckled in spite of myself.

It was Seamus's turn to laugh. "Why?"

I shrugged into the phone. "Don't you think thirty's a little old for a twenty-five-year-old?"

"To be truthful, I thought you were my age, but now that you tell me, it doesn't bother me." I mentally gave him points for thinking I was his age, but I wasn't sold yet. And I had no idea what to say.

Seamus continued, "So, I'm twenty-five and you're thirty, so let's just round it to somewhere in the middle and say we're both twenty-seven. What do you think?"

I think I liked it, because, against my will, I liked Seamus. I mean, he was five years younger and a foreigner who'd probably end up going back to his homeland, but I always did go for the underdog. I sighed, and then I laughed. "Okay."

"Great, so we're on for Friday night, right?"

Yes, yes, we were.

At the end of the month, I'd moved into the Parkside apartment with Marie. Seamus helped move me in and even put together all of my massive Crate & Barrel furniture. *How sweet,* I thought. That's why, when I moved back home a month later, I felt slightly guilty, but only slightly. The new living arrangement just wasn't working out, and it had nothing to do with Marie. It was all me.

For starters, I was never there. With the exception of work, my family, my friends, and the gym were all closer to where I'd lived before. And then there was Seamus, who lived in that area, as well. When I did stay at the apartment, I felt like I was staying at a hotel, a nice hotel, but it never felt like home. I was there to sleep, or maybe eat, or leave for work. I wasn't there to stay. But that's the way I am. If I lived at home, I was never there either. I was visiting friends or going up to the city. When I lived in the city, I was always coming home. I know. *I know.* I have definite adjustment issues.

That said, I was not willing to pay rent for a place in which I hardly stayed. And another key deciding factor—Seamus had made it apparent from the beginning that he didn't care if I lived at home. Although I had told myself time and time again that it shouldn't matter what people thought, I had always believed myself to be nondatable while living at home. It finally was clear that I didn't need to prove anything by moving out, and it was an absolute relief. And now I could also go back to getting my expensive facials.

So, Seamus picked up the U-Haul truck, disassembled the furniture he had so thoughtfully put together, packed me up, and moved me back home. When I happened to mention to my mom that I wanted to repaint my room, Seamus volunteered to do it for me on one of his days off. And he did. If the air in my tires looked low (so I was practically driving on my rims—what was the big deal?), he took my car to the gas station and filled the tires. If he had extra wood from a job he was doing, he'd show up with something he'd made for me. The first was a three-tiered CD shelf. I couldn't get over it. He was always doing stuff for me.

And he still continued to devotedly show up for Sunday dinner at Grandma's. Between the time he spent with me at my mom's and at Grandma's, it was like having a new family member. Mom and Grandma loved it, but I could sense my sister's irritation, not that she was obvious about it or anything. "Ugh, he's coming over *again*?" she'd utter before stomping out of the room.

I wasn't sure what my sister's problem was with Seamus. He was perfectly nice to her, and she had yet to bring up getting any of her bad vibes from him, so I couldn't understand it.

"What's her problem?" I asked my mom.

My mom shook her head and shrugged. "Oh, I just think she misses hanging out with you. You're not home a lot, and when you are, Seamus is too. She'll get over it. I hope."

I did too, yet at the same time, I didn't care. I was going to date Seamus whether my sister or anybody else liked it. I liked him, and if his actions meant anything at all, the feeling was mutual. And I don't need to tell you, a girl can really get used to all that unsolicited attention. The best part was I never even had to ask for it. It was all Seamus.

Before I knew it, two months had flown by. Seamus and I were out to dinner at a local Mexican joint. Over the tortilla chips he grabbed my hand and asked, "Giuliana, where have you been all my life?"

Where I'd always been, here, home. For once I was glad I wasn't much of a gallivanting wanderer.

I swallowed the tortilla chip that had almost become lodged in my throat and shrugged. Then clearing my throat, I said, "Just … here, I guess."

He smiled and said, "Well, lucky me for finding you. So, how do you feel about having a boyfriend?"

Hmm. I was not sure how to proceed in this conversation. Did he mean how did I feel about having a boyfriend in general? Like, overall, in a nutshell, was it a good or a bad thing? Or was he implying that he considered himself my boyfriend, and how did I feel about that? I fervently hoped it was the latter, or this was going to be quite awkward.

"Um, I don't know. They don't usually last more than a month or so," I said drolly. This was true. For whatever reason (i.e., I didn't like them enough or they didn't like me enough), my past suitors never survived the six-week mark.

Seamus winked at me and said, "It's been well over a month, so I guess this is a good sign. Shall we continue?"

Whoa, he's asking to be my boyfriend. I would've preferred him to actually say, "I'd like to be your boyfriend. It's just you and me, kid, from now on," since I'm forever fearful of assuming the wrong thing in matters of the heart, but I guessed this was good enough. Should we continue (a.k.a. should he), could he be my boyfriend?

"Yes," I answered.

"Good," he said. God, I loved his accent. I think I might've even loved him at that point. It was a done deal. I was so in it. I had an Irish boyfriend. *Yippee!*

We hit the six-month mark. To me that was pretty big, considering my dating record. I was happy. We were happy. We spent all our time together. I still did things with my friends, because I'm not the type of girl to ditch her friends for a guy. But Seamus didn't seem to have many close friends, so he ended up hanging out with me and my friends most of the time anyway. I wondered why he didn't have a plethora of Irish buddies to hang out with, since the local Irish network was so strong. He knew a lot of people, of course, but we never did much with any of the Irish. If we ever went out to the local Irish bars, we'd chat with people, but I never really got to know any of them. I would have liked to, but Seamus would always comment, "Oh, I hate that one. He's a feckin' eejit!"

"Feckin' eejit" means "fuckin' idiot" for all you non-Irish speakers. Feckin' and fuckin' are quite common staples in the Irish vocabulary, just so you know.

"Why?" I'd ask. Everyone I met seemed pretty nice.

"Oh, he just is. I could tell you stories," he'd grumble. But he never really did. It was the same with the Irish women, who I was dying to get to know. Seamus had a comment for everyone. "Your one there, don't ever talk to her. She's awful, she is. A feckin' liar!"

"Um, okay." I'd try to look sideways at the supposedly evil Irish girl at the end of the bar who was drinking with her friends to see if the horns growing out of her head and her pitchfork were showing. She seemed normal, but what did I know? Josie was my only Irish friend, and she didn't spend a lot of time in the Irish bars. I knew none of these people whom Seamus complained about or forbade me to have anything to do with. I assumed he was just being protective.

However, I cringed whenever he made cruel remarks about random passersby (Irish or not), which happened quite a lot. "God, look at her. A real pig in lipstick!"

He'd laugh, but I wouldn't. "That's mean," I'd say.

"It's not mean. It's true," he answered matter-of-factly.

Another favorite expression of Seamus's was "Ugh, she's got a face like a fur hatchet!" I wasn't sure what a face like a fur hatchet looked like. Did the poor girl in question resemble Chewbacca and need to wax her face or something? I didn't know, but I guessed it wasn't good.

"Jeez, I'd hate to hear what you say when I leave the room!" I joked. But for once, Seamus didn't have a comment. He just shrugged at me. I wasn't sure if that was good or bad. Yes, I noticed that Seamus was a little on the critical side. And we bickered quite a bit. It was playful bickering, like an old married couple, but I wondered if that was normal. I had nothing to judge it against. My parents had split when I was six, and the only male figure in my life had been my grandfather. And he and my grandmother were always annoying each other to no end. We were all quite used to hearing Gramps mutter under his breath that he was "living in a nightmare," usually when he'd had to repeat something for the zillionth time because Grandma's hearing aids weren't working. While this all was quite the norm in our family, it didn't mean I was okay with it.

"Is this normal, us fighting all the time?" I finally asked Seamus.

"Of course it is, and we're not really fighting anyway," he'd answer assuredly. I didn't agree but guessed that Seamus really couldn't help it. His father was an alcoholic, and Seamus, along with his siblings and his mother, all despised him. Apparently, his parents had both taken the pledge to never drink before they wed, but as luck would have it, his dad started hitting the bottle as soon as they married. Seamus had countless drunken stories of his father. I listened with utter sadness as Seamus told me about all the Christmases his dad would stumble in from a drinking tear, scream at the kids, and break all their new toys. Or he'd be gone drinking for three days and return to rant incoherently at the family. Seamus's mother, Geraldine, would finally have enough of it and start hurling hot baked potatoes at his head till he'd leave the house again.

Poor Seamus. No wonder he was so critical. Therefore, I felt I couldn't say too much. I guessed that anyone who thought launching baked potatoes at someone's noggin was normal adult interaction would assuredly think much calmer bickering was just fine. But it worried me. While I wasn't sure what 100 percent normal relationships looked like, this didn't feel completely right to me.

So Seamus lacked a big group of friends, and the Irish ladies weren't clambering to initiate me into their tight circle. No huge deal. My family and friends had welcomed Seamus in, and he was happy with it. In fact, my family and friends were the only people Seamus didn't rag on. Seamus might not be perfect, but no one was, I reasoned. And when you love someone, their imperfections seem like nothing more than endearing little quirks anyway.

Yes, I loved him. I loved him and was in up to my eyeballs in love with him. I told him so. And he was in love with me. Yeah, he told me so. No, I really wasn't imagining or assuming anything. We said it. And we'd even talked about marriage. Where might we live? And all that sort of stuff. And it all was brought up by Seamus, not me. Yes, all signs pointed to this relationship heading in a most serious and long-term direction. Seamus had my whole heart. I had his. And of course, that's when it all started to unravel, or, as some of us like to say, the shit hit the ceiling fan at full force.

We were lying around watching TV at Seamus's one Saturday night, when Seamus looked at me and nervously said, "Giuliana, I have something to ask you."

My heart pounded. My mind, as it will typically do, suddenly jumped to ridiculous conclusions. *He isn't going to propose to me, is he? Damn it, I wish I had my hair blown out and I wasn't wearing my workout sweats.* But how typical. I had to give it to Seamus. If this was it, he was certainly catching me off guard. But wait, I was completely getting ahead of myself. Still, I was quite suddenly and extremely nervous. I could literally feel the hairs on my arm standing up. I mean, marriage was a huge step. I loved Seamus, and we'd talked about it and all, but I didn't know if I was ready for matrimony so soon. I looked sideways at him and said hesitatingly, "Okay …"

"I don't know how to ask you, but …" His voice trailed off, and he looked down bashfully. Huddled next to me, he then looked up at me with what now didn't seem to be bashfulness but actual dread. I thought in the best-case scenario no one who was about to propose should appear absolutely horrified—perhaps a little worried, but not like he was a dead man walking. *Hmm. Well?* I wondered, practically on the edge of my seat. What else could he possibly be going to ask me?

I waited. He looked up and said meekly, "Would you be able to help me buy a car?"

What? I thought.

"What?" I shouted out loud, as if he was asking me for a kidney, which he might as well have been. I had no extra funds of that sort lying around. What did he need a car for, what with the lovely silver Mercedes he already had?

"A new car? Why?" I asked, baffled. Then again, maybe Seamus had a good reason. Maybe he was going to get rid of the Mercedes so he could get a truck for work. Yes, that was probably it. *How responsible and practical of him,* I thought with relief.

"Well, I really want to trade in my car …" he began.

Yes? I waited for his answer.

"For a CLA-Class," he finished.

I had no idea what the hell a CLA-Class was. "What's a CLA-Class?" I asked dumbly.

"It's a Mercedes," he answered.

Really? There went all thoughts of responsibility or practicality.

"But you *have* a Mercedes," I said.

However, I had a feeling I was preaching to the choir. "It's not the same, Giuliana. The CLA-Class is much, much nicer. And it's faster."

"Faster? What, are you planning on drag racing?" I scoffed at the ridiculous notion.

Seamus rolled his eyes at me and then launched into all the other reasons he "needed" to have this car. I couldn't tell you what they were, since they had to do with the engine and other random, so-called amazing doohickeys. I couldn't have cared less. If the car had a drink holder and air-conditioning (unlike my own), I considered it quite luxurious. Who really cared about the rest?

When he was finished, he sat quietly, staring at me nervously with those piercing blue eyes of his. I had to hand it to him—his argument was very well-thought-out, with an overabundance of research-based evidence as to why he had to have the CLA-Class, not that I remembered any of it. Despite my first impulse to say no, I was impressed.

I suddenly realized that his car spiel was akin to every discussion I'd ever had with my mother, or any heated argument any female has ever had with their significant other as to why they've "needed" and purchased another pair of black shoes. "Because this one has a square heel, and my others are spiked." "Because it's patent leather." "Because it has a bow." "Because it's open-toed." "Because it's versatile and can be worn with jeans or a dress." "Because … it's nothing I can explain. I … just want them." I know I have a list of reasons that could span the ages. Yes, Seamus and I had just had the men's version of the black pair of shoes talk. And I totally got him. But I did not have that kind of money. Shelling out hundreds of dollars on a good pair of shoes is quite different from the thousands of dollars necessary for a new car. And I was fairly sure that this Mercedes would cost more than I made in a single year of teaching. That was a lot of potential shoes, among other necessary things.

"Okay, but, Seamus, I don't have that kind of money," I said apologetically.

"I don't really need the money. What I need is credit. See, I've got bad credit. But if your credit is good, you could help cosign for the car," he explained earnestly.

I didn't know if I had good credit. I had a little bit of debt, but I paid my bills on time every month. I didn't think to ask Seamus why he didn't have good credit. I guess I figured it was none of my business, and what did it matter at that point?

"Explain this cosigning thing," I said warily.

He answered, "So if you cosign, then we'd both have our names on the pink slip as owners of the car."

My radar was up at once. "But I don't want to own this car. I have a car, one that's completely paid for. I'm not helping with monthly car payments." I folded my arms. I would not be throwing good shoe/clothing/facial money into monthly car payments for a car that I didn't want.

"You won't make the car payments. I will. And we won't keep your name on the car. After a month or so, I'll have your name removed, and sole ownership will be transferred to me. You won't have to worry about a thing. I just need … you … to help sign for the car. That's all, I swear." Seamus looked at me hopefully.

I wouldn't make car payments. Good. The car would not remain in my name. Good. Was this a stupid idea? Probably. Did I love Seamus? Definitely. Why was it wrong to help someone you loved and who loved you? It wasn't, and it was my prerogative to do so or to not do so.

"Okay." I smiled at him, almost feeling like a parent indulging her begging child.

"Okay? Really?" He looked shocked. I nodded my head yes.

Seamus threw his arms around me and kissed me. "I love you, Giuliana. Thank you." Loved me? I thought so. I hoped so.

Apparently, according to Bob, who ran the credit check at the Mercedes dealership, I had excellent credit. Who knew? I was quite happy to know I had more than decent credit, and Seamus, of course, was almost giddy. We signed some papers. Bob explained the monthly payment of $640. I almost fell over until I remembered that thankfully, I wasn't making those ridiculous monthly payments. Seamus was. I'd have to remind him in a month to have my name taken off the papers.

And then it was time. Bob handed Seamus the keys to the black Mercedes CLA-Class, and we climbed aboard. As Seamus revved the engine in macho delight and backed up, Bob waved and called out, "Congratulations! Good luck. Call me if you need anything!" It was as if we were two newlyweds embarking upon our honeymoon. I watched Bob become smaller in the side-view mirror and sighed. If only I'd known this was literally the beginning of the end for Seamus and me.

Spring came around, and that meant so did Gaelic Football. From what I could make of it from the times I'd seen Seamus play, the sport seemed a cross between American football and rugby. Like football, there was some sort of ball. And like rugby, the guys wore rugby-type shirts and no protective gear at all. And that's about the extent of the information I can give you about it. Ask me anything about American football or baseball, but Gaelic football was literally foreign to me.

Anyway, it's a pretty big deal for the Irish community in the Bay Area. Women's and men's teams from the San Francisco Bay Area compete each Sunday, ending with a championship around Labor Day.

Seamus played for one of the city teams and, from what I heard from Josie and her husband, was pretty sought after among the local teams for being such a good player. I'd only seen him play a couple of times and was excited to watch more as the season progressed. I figured it'd be fun to support Seamus and one of his hobbies, since God knew he didn't do much else but work and golf.

Work was a given, and I wasn't invited to golf or really to do anything else. In fact, Seamus no longer feigned polite or any interest in coming with me to functions and get-togethers that involved my friends. Oh, there was always a reason. He was too tired, he had to finish up a job, he was golfing with the couple friends he actually had, or he just preferred hanging with me alone. I didn't mind doing things on my own with my friends, and my friends never interrogated me over the reasons Seamus was absent, so I left it at that. But I was often left wondering what was the point of actually having a boyfriend if he never wanted to do anything or go anywhere with you. Dilemmas.

Therefore, I was looking forward to Gaelic football. I'd actually get to spend time with Seamus in a different environment. So I was taken aback when Seamus announced matter-of-factly, "I won't be seeing you on Sundays because of football, and I'm not gonna be coming to your grandmother's for dinner anymore."

I'd heard incorrectly, hadn't I?

"Ever?" I asked incredulously. I knew I was prone to be dramatic, but really? He had to be joking. This was the guy, my so-called boyfriend, who'd been coming of his own free will to Sunday dinner since before we'd officially even become a couple. And I guessed that meant I wasn't invited to his games either. I couldn't hide the disappointment on my face.

"Look, Giuliana, I have football on Sunday, and I won't have time anymore to be coming over," he said succinctly to me, as if I was one of the passengers on the short bus.

"Ever? I can understand if you can't make it to dinner all the time, but *never, at all*?" I argued.

"Look, I'm not coming anymore," Seamus said, his voice rising.

I didn't understand why he was so adamant about this. Where was this coming from? And how were my mom and grandma going to take this? I looked at him without saying anything. They would surely take it as a personal rejection. My sister would probably jump for joy, since it was becoming clearer as time passed that she didn't like Seamus, but that really wasn't the issue at hand.

"What?" he asked scornfully.

"Well, you've been coming to Sunday dinner for months. And now you're just *never* going to come anymore? I think my mom and grandma will think you don't like them anymore ... or something," I answered. I didn't know why I felt like I was defending myself, as if I was guilty.

"I do like them, and that's not my problem." He looked at me defiantly. "Besides, I never said I was always going to come for Sunday dinner."

I could feel my throat tightening in anger. "I know you never said you were always coming for dinner, but you *did,* and that was your choice, by the way. So, you can tell my mom and grandmother that you're no longer coming to dinner anymore."

Seamus shook his head. "You tell them." And he left.

I was pissed. It was one thing to be rude to me, which, by the way, I wasn't okay with, but I'd deal with it on my own terms. It was another thing to blow off my mother and grandmother, who'd done nothing but welcome Seamus in like a long-lost family member.

When I broke the news to the ladies, there was an awkward silence. Grandma shrugged and said, "Oh, well, that's too bad."

But Mom wasn't so convincing. "Hmm." She raised her eyebrows and shrugged.

"Well, the games last all day, and they're up in the city, so by the time Seamus gets back, it'll be late. He wouldn't want us to be waiting around to eat," I said hastily. I didn't know why I was defending him, perhaps to protect my mom's and grandma's feelings.

"Oh, that's all right. Tell him we can wait for him," Grandma said hopefully. This was awful. I cursed Seamus for making me be the bearer of bad news. I cringed and said, "No, no, just don't worry about him coming for dinner on Sundays, Grandma."

Later, when my sister heard, she immediately threw in her two cents, as I expected. "Humph, I don't like him."

"No, *really*?" I said sarcastically. "And you're just telling me now?"

Annie shrugged and said, "There's just something about him. I don't trust him. And Brendan doesn't like him either."

Brendan was my sister's relatively new boyfriend that she spent every waking moment with. He was Irish too. In fact, she'd only met him because I'd dragged her out (against her will) with Seamus and me to O'Hooley's one night. Brendan was a plumber and had worked on contracting jobs with Seamus, and he'd introduced the two of them at Brendan's request. I thought it was a little unfair of my sister and her beau to ungratefully judge, when Seamus and I had been the reason they'd met in the first place. But whatever.

"Well, I'm sorry you and Brendan don't like Seamus, but you're not dating him," I said snootily.

"Right, so just be careful. I just ... I don't know. I don't like him. And he looks like Curious George with those stupid ears that stick out!" Annie sniggered a little too enthusiastically.

I snorted at the absurdity and immaturity of her comment (even though there was a slight resemblance, but still, she was speaking rudely of my boyfriend). "Well, we can't all be perfect now, can we?" I said drolly.

"No, but at least I have small ears," my sister chimed in. I couldn't argue with her on that one. She did have tiny ears.

"Right, it's a wonder you can hear anything at all!" I stomped off, knowing I'd never win that conversation, whether it was about Seamus's ears or his unfavorable (according to Annie) personality. In fact, after the "no Sunday dinner" manifesto, I couldn't win anything with Seamus either.

The stupid bickering continued nonstop, and there was no pleasing him either. If, perchance, I dressed up even just slightly to go out (and mind you, we'd only be going to the movies or to whichever local Irish bar wasn't on Seamus's shit list at the moment), he'd glance at me sideways and comment, "Why are you so dressed up? Where do you think we're going?"

"I was hoping for something more along the lines of 'Wow, you look nice,'" I said flatly. He'd laugh and shrug, yet if I came out in jeans, it was a critical stare and a "Why don't you ever dress up, wear some high-heeled boots or something nice?"

"Well, that would be because we never go anywhere!" I screamed in frustration.

With Seamus I was never right. And all I needed and wanted was just some kind of positive affirmation, any kind of tiny inkling of his actually still wanting to be with me, other than that he was just there with nothing better to do. I tried to understand him. I wanted to understand him, to give him the benefit of the doubt. After all, he was the product of a very broken and dysfunctional home, but still. I came from a technically "broken" family, but I was what I considered a relatively pleasant person most of the time, although my sister might have begged to differ.

Besides his constant negativity, the only thing that was becoming predictable about Seamus was his unpredictability. We'd been dating for almost two and a half years, and he had us walking on eggshells. And when I say "us," I mean my whole family. With every holiday, birthday, or special happening came some sort of trauma caused by Seamus.

Things would typically go like this: The day of some big event would be upon us (insert event of choice: Christmas, Easter, the huge twenty-fifth anniversary party for my mom thrown by the school she worked for, or the crème de la crème—my birthday). It really didn't matter what it was. Seamus would call at the absolute last minute and tell me he wasn't coming for whatever reason. Oh, it was always something: he was sick, he was working (on Christmas Eve at 5:00 p.m.? I didn't think so), or perchance he had to go to a Rosary for an Irish guy (whom I'd never heard him speak of). And that was rare, since he had something to say about everybody—and mostly unfavorable, as well. Yes, the said Rosary was on my birthday, of course. The Rosary conveniently coincided with the birthday dinner I was having with my family. And, no, there was no way he could stop by after to join us all for dessert. But I could certainly meet up with him and others at O'Hooley's, and he'd give me my present then.

I was hurt. This was my birthday. I was mad. *This was my birthday.* Don't fuck with birthdays, at least not mine. I was tired of this nonsense. The relationship had been going south for quite some time. He'd constantly blow off something that he knew was important to me. Upset, I'd cry over it, and then I'd suggest taking a break from each other. It seemed the logical thing to do. Perhaps he wanted to date other people. It sure as hell didn't seem like he wanted to date me. And really, in the back of my mind, while I didn't want us to be over, I was hoping he'd say yes, because I was worn-out. I just couldn't do it anymore.

Then he'd cry (yes, actually cry tears) and tell me he was so sorry. He didn't want to date anyone else, just me. *Really?* That was odd. I suppose he was using the old reverse psychology. I would be so taken aback seeing him cry and hearing him apologize that I'd accept his apology and things would be fine for a while, Seamus being very contrite and all. Then the same shit would happen all over again.

This was the last straw. *Go down to O'Hooley's so I could get my birthday gift?* Oh, I was going. You bet your motherfucking Irish ass I was. There I go again with the swearing. So sorry, but I was riled up. Not only was I furious, but I was on the verge of tears (again), because Seamus was *mean.* There was no other way to say it. I was dating (if you could call it that anymore) a very mean and manipulative person who just really sucked. There were no two ways about it anymore. He clearly and obviously and blatantly and totally redundantly sucked. And I was finally able to admit that which I'd been trying to ignore for far too long. So, on to O'Hooley's!

I flounced into O'Hooley's (if it's possible to flounce into such an establishment). His back was to me as he stood talking to a bunch of Irish guys. I was greeted first by the Irish "Norm" of the bar. Like Norm of *Cheers,* he always commandeered one corner of the bar. That was his specific place, and it was completely creepy if anyone else was in it or if, God forbid, he wasn't there. But that never happened. I'm pretty sure he was always there, spouting out Irish intellectual witticisms. I tell you, the man was scary smart. Almost everything he said was over my head, but only because it's hard to understand drunken slurring in an Irish accent. Yet he was always singing my praises, telling me what a great girl I was, so he was forever okay in my book.

However, that night I was not in the mood for conversational shenanigans with Irish Norm. "Well, hello, Giuliana! And I hear it's your birthday too. Happy birthday to you!" said Irish Norm grandly.

I gave him my fake half smile and a very bitchy "Thanks."

He shrugged and mumbled toward the bar, "Jesus! Well, who took the jelly out of her doughnut?"

Seamus turned around. "Hi there. How was your dinner?" *How was my dinner? How about how was my f'ing birthday, a-hole?*

"Great," I said icily. "How was the Rosary?"

Ignoring my frostiness, Seamus shook his head. "Aw, there were a lot of people there. Everyone cryin' and all. Was pretty bad." I wanted to punch him in his Irish nose for his fake forlornness. He had missed my birthday for the Rosary of someone he wasn't even friends with, someone he barely knew. Was I being selfish? I didn't think so.

"Want a drink?" he asked blandly.

"No. In fact, I'm leaving," I said. This was so stupid. He was so stupid.

"Leaving? Well, walk with me to my car. I have your present," he said, and he didn't seem too disappointed I wasn't sticking around either. I should've said right then and there, "Screw you and your present!" and hightailed it out. Honestly, I couldn't stand him anymore, but the truth was I did want the present. Believe me, if anyone deserved a present, it was me. I mean, for all I'd put up with, I deserved the likes of something à la Miu Miu or, say, Cartier. Hence, I followed.

We walked a block to his beloved CLA-Class, and he reached in and pulled out a small box. It was sized just right for some type of jewelry. Seamus had already bought me a beautiful white gold cross and chain our first Christmas together, when he'd actually liked me. I wondered what this could be. I admit there was a small bit of hope fluttering around inside me. Maybe he was truly sorry for all the times he'd hurt me. Maybe he was going to make it up to me with a really nice piece of jewelry. A ring? Maybe this was a new start. I had kind of been joking about the Cartier, but not really.

I unwrapped the box. It wasn't the dreamy Cartier box. Instead, it was from the local Irish store that sold crystal, jewelry, and other fine Irish goods. *Okay,* I wondered, *is it a claddagh ring?* I opened the box. Inside lay—drumroll, please—a pair of silver shamrock earrings. Yeah, you heard me right.

Quite lovely, if you were, say, about eight years old or even eighty years old. To the earrings' credit, they did have pavé diamonds, but *shamrocks*? Really? I only wore plain diamond studs that I never took out. This was something a tourist would buy sightseeing in Dublin. This was not something you bought your thirty-three-year-old girlfriend of almost three years. Did Seamus not know me at all?

I bit my lip in an effort to contain my disappointment and lividness. "Um, they're … nice," I said in a very monotone voice.

"Oh, for fuck's sake, Giuliana! I spent five hundred dollars on those! You're so fucking ungrateful!" And he ripped the box out of my hand and threw it across the darkened parking lot.

Ungrateful for a piece-of-crap present? Why, yes, I was. I also knew my jewelry, and if we were really going to go tit for tat, there was absolutely no way in hell he'd spent five hundred dollars on those stupid earrings.

"Oh, five hundred dollars and you throw them off into the middle of a dark parking lot? Wow, that seems like a waste of money to me. I'd be looking for those and returning them," I said stoically as I backed away, lest he decide he might like to hurl something at the back of my head. Seamus stared at me with a look of utter disgust and stormed off in the direction in which he'd chucked the loathsome earrings.

I walked away as fast as I could. When I got to my car, I locked myself in and cried. I didn't mean this in the slightest materialistic way at all, but I thought I was worth a hell of a lot more than a pair of tacky earrings. It was truly and in the most clichéd way the thought that counted, and there had clearly been no thought. I guess I wasn't surprised, but it still hurt.

The next day Seamus called in the late afternoon.

"Look, I'm not going to come to dinner tonight." No shocker given the hideous earring-throwing incident of the previous night and the fact that this was the night a group of my friends were taking me out for my birthday, so of course he'd bail.

"Okay," I answered dully.

"And I think we should stop seeing each other for a while," he said seriously.

"Fine with me," I answered coolly. And it really was.

He paused for a moment before saying with slight disbelief, "Oh, um, okay."

I would strike while the iron was hot. If it was over, I wanted to know for certain so I could make a clean break and be done with it all. "So it's fine to see other people and all that?" I assumed Seamus wouldn't possibly have any objections and would most likely be jumping for joy on his end of the phone.

"Giuli, I don't want to see other people. *I'm* not going to be seeing other people," Seamus answered emphatically. "Are you?" he asked, as if I was plotting to run out and hook up with the first random guy I could find.

"No," I answered, as if insulted. I didn't want to see anyone. I didn't want to see Seamus either. Well, let's rephrase. I wanted the Seamus I'd fallen in love with. I wanted the guy who'd loved me and doted on me and who'd actually wanted to spend all his time with me, whether alone or with my family. Yeah, I wanted that guy back. I knew he was in there somewhere. I didn't know what had happened or when, but I'd have taken that Seamus back in a heartbeat. So, to your dismay, I'm sure, hearing Seamus say he didn't want to see anyone had created some type of hope, at least for the time being.

"Giuli," he said imploringly, "neither of us'll see anyone. I just need some time to myself to make some more money, get all my shit straightened out, and then things will be fine with us, okay?"

How much money did he need? He'd already borrowed quite a bit from me to pay off some debts. He'd yet to pay me back. Would things be fine? I didn't know.

"Fine," I said. We hung up. I cried some more. This annoying crying thing was becoming a regular occurrence. Maybe now it would subside for a while.

I didn't call him. I didn't go into the local Irish bars. I felt there was no need to check up on him or know what he was up to. I'd never had reason to doubt Seamus before. He may have been a jerk, but he'd never lied to me.

However, it was Seamus who called me, at least a few days every week. We even went out to dinner a couple of times. And it was lovely, we had lots to talk about, and there was no pressure. I was still on guard, though. Other than a quick peck good-bye, I didn't kiss him. I didn't go back to his place. I wanted to, but I always made sure that if we saw each other it was on a work night, when I'd have to get home to go to sleep early. I wasn't sure what was going on with us, but it seemed like a step in the right direction. Seamus wanted to see me, and we had nothing to fight about.

It was Valentine's Day. Seamus called, as was his routine.

"Some of the girls and I are going for drinks. Want to join us?" I asked. I've never been big on Valentine's Day, as it is overcommercialized and always makes singles feel like they're total losers, but I couldn't help but feel wistful about seeing Seamus.

"Where are you going?" he asked.

"Out in town." I mentioned the bar.

"Aw, thanks, but I think I'll be staying in tonight. Have to work early tomorrow," Seamus answered. "I'll talk to you this week, though."

I was disappointed, I admit. But we were taking a break from each other, and he wasn't seeing anyone else, so I couldn't be too upset.

He was seeing someone else. Yes, I'm sure you had your suspicions long before I ever did. In my defense though, it's only because you weren't blindly in love with Seamus. That's the only reason that you're so smugly smart. Maybe. Okay, I'm trying to make myself feel better.

The next day my sister came into the bathroom as I was blow-drying my hair. "Hey, I need to tell you something," she said in a serious tone. It doesn't matter how anyone actually says, "I need to tell you something." It's never going to be good. I turned the hair dryer off. My stomach jumped slightly as I waited apprehensively.

"Brendan and I were at O'Hooley's last night, and Seamus was there." She paused. "With a girl. He's apparently been dating her for over a month. I just wanted you to know." Her voice trailed off.

My heart was pounding. *Over a month?* That's when we'd decided to take a break—a break where we weren't supposed to be seeing other people. I guess I'd somehow gotten it all wrong. I wasn't to see other people, but it was okay for Seamus to do so.

"What? Who? Are you sure?" I asked dumbly.

Annie answered, "She's American, some tall blonde girl who works at that Irish British store in Burlington. Apparently, word in the bar is that according to him, she's his new girlfriend. And according to him, he's been trying to get rid of you for a while, but you just wouldn't let go. His words."

What? I wasn't some pathetic loser who'd been trying to hang onto him! I'd wanted to end it so many times, but Seamus had been the one to say no. *How dare he!* I had no questions and yet so, so many.

"What? I can't believe this. I asked him if he wanted to go out with me and the girls last night, and he said no, he was staying in. He had to work today. Well, did he see you?" I asked, my voice slightly frantic.

"Oh, he saw me. And as soon as he did, he acted like he wasn't with her and came right over and said hello in his stupid, weasely voice. The he went back to her and kind of pushed her to the back of the bar. Then they left out the back. And by the way, she's about two inches taller than him. He looked ridiculous!" Annie spit out in disgust.

Unfortunately, I got no satisfaction from the fact that she was taller than him. I was humiliated. He'd lied to me. He'd lied *about* me and made me seem like I was a delusional loser. He could've said he wanted to see other people. Why hadn't he? And had he met this floozy (I chose to think of her as a floozy since it made me feel better) when he was out buying my ugly birthday gift? That was just adding insult to injury. Had she helped him pick it out? And hadn't she figured out he must have a girlfriend if he was buying jewelry that was somewhat expensive? Then again, the earrings weren't exactly hip and sexy. He probably told her he was buying them for his mother back home. That would have seemed completely plausible. Oh, the shame! My mind whirled with a thousand thoughts at a time. What to do? What to do?

"Are you okay? I'm so sorry. I—I just thought you should know. Be done with him. He's a complete loser, Giuliana," Annie said, putting a hand on my shoulder.

I looked at her almost blankly and said, "Yeah, I guess so."

"What are you going to do? Are you going to say something?" she asked.

"Oh, I'll say something. He still owes me money. But I'll wait till he calls."

The very next day Seamus called. I knew he would. He was going to call to see if I'd heard anything.

"How was your night out?" he asked pleasantly.

"Oh, it was great. How was your night?" I asked just as cheerfully.

"Oh, I just watched some TV and went to bed. So are you up for dinner tonight?" he asked.

"Sure," I said. I had no intention of eating dinner with him.

"Would you mind picking me up in Burlington, by the train station? I had to drop my car off near there for some repairs."

"Sure," I answered. "Oh, and by the way, bring at least half the money you owe me, okay?" I said in a steely voice.

"Um, okay," he answered with slight trepidation. "Great," I answered and hung up before he could say anything else. I wanted my money and to tell him off, and then we'd be done—that is, if he showed up.

I sat parked at the train station and anxiously waited for him. He finally walked up and smiled as I unlocked the door for him to get in. "Hello," he said.

"Hi," I said shortly. "Do you have my money?" I cut to the chase.

"Uh, yeah, well, I just have a thousand. That's all I can do for right now," he said in a small voice and handed me an envelope. I peeked inside and counted the cash. I hoped no random police officers would wander by and think we were finishing a drug deal. I counted out a thousand. It wasn't even a third of what he owed me, but it would do for now. I looked up to see Seamus watching me nervously. I think it was fair to say he knew something was up.

"So," I said, "how was your Valentine's Day, really? You know, with your new girlfriend?"

"W—what?" he asked in fake bewilderedness.

Seriously, did he think I was a moron? By the way, that was strictly a rhetorical question.

"Oh, don't lie. My sister already told me she saw you two at O'Hooley's," I said disgustedly.

Seamus rolled his eyes. "She's just a friend. Look, she asked me out. She's a total airhead anyway!"

I snorted. "That's no way to talk about your girlfriend," I answered snappily. My heart was breaking, but I had to admit I was still enjoying having the upper hand.

"She's not my girlfriend! I'm not seeing *anyone*," he said, annoyed and too huffily.

I fumed. I was the wronged party in this scenario.

"*Right.* Get out," I said.

"What?" he said stupidly.

"You know, you could've just said you wanted to see other people. You lied to me and made me look like a complete jackass!" I yelled.

"Look," he began.

"Get out!" I said, "And don't forget about the rest of the money you owe me, because I won't."

He stared at me for a moment or two before hanging his head down dejectedly and saying, "Okay." For a second it looked as if Seamus was going to try pulling his crying act, but I nipped that in the bud with a harsh "*Good-bye.*"

He got out and closed the door. I made a screeching U-turn in the empty parking lot and blew past Seamus as he stared sadly at me. I think he was saying something, but I ignored him and drove away. He was an idiot. I knew it. As soon as I was far enough away, I cried anyway.

I was devastated, but it was a much more elevated state of devastation, nothing like when Dante Prosecco unwittingly fractured my heart. This was pure brokenness. I was completely broken, and the pain was so much greater. And then there was the embarrassment and the humiliation on top of that. How long had Seamus been going around telling people that we were just friends and that he was trying to shake me, like some annoying piece of lint from a fuzzy sweater? Yeah, the humiliation was at the core of my devastation. And then came the anger and the hurt of being betrayed. I had never placed my complete trust in a man before. I'd never let myself, until Seamus. And look at what happened.

And then there was just pure sadness. What was wrong with me? Wasn't I good enough for a working-class boy from Tyrone? Wasn't I pretty enough, smart enough? Or was I too pretty? I doubted it. Was I too smart? Probably, although that didn't make me feel better. Did I need to lose weight? For sure, since I'd put on some pounds dating Seamus. I am of petite stature by nature. And what I mean is I'm short, no more than five feet one. For some reason I decided that at that point in time, the only thing I could change was my weight. And focus on it I did, like a madwoman.

By the time the summer rolled around, I was only 104 pounds. Absolutely tiny. As soon as I'd eat, I'd hop on the treadmill in the garage and run till I burned off the calories I'd just eaten, unless I was at work. It was ridiculous. Of course, I still drank like a fish when I went out with friends. But at least I was a lightweight now. A couple of drinks and I was ready to pass out. If you were to suggest that I was borderline having an eating/drinking disorder, I wouldn't disagree with you.

However, I can't tell you how many times I've tried to recreate the Seamus weight-loss plan since (minus the Seamus part, of course), but it never comes close to being as successful. No matter how depressed or upset I am, I can't manage to ever completely lose my appetite for more than an hour or so or to fiendishly work out. Apparently I've never been in such stupefied anguish, which I suppose is a very good thing, but still.

So in July I took my depressed 106-pound (I'd managed to gain a couple of pounds) self to Italy with my high school friend Kit. It seemed the thing to do that summer. I needed an escape. I couldn't go anywhere without running into people, Irish or not, who had stories (all bad) to tell about Seamus—lies he'd told, money he owed, crap he'd said about me, and how much *nobody* had ever liked him. If I heard one more random Irish person exclaim vehemently, "Oh God, I can't stand that guy!" I was going to scream and not because I wanted to defend Seamus but because I wondered why no one had ever said anything to me. "If I'd only known" became my new and overly used mantra.

Suffice it to say, I still felt like quite the village idiot. Leaving the country, as well as avoiding the possibility of running into Seamus and his on-again/off-again taller-than-him, blonde, Amazon girlfriend who worked in the Irish store, sounded ideal. I had a fabulous time in Italy and managed to drown my sorrows quite well in prosecco and wine. Oh, and some cute boys too, which was a much-needed, if only temporary, ego boost. And somehow, somehow, I gained back a few shreds of my tattered self-esteem. Not much, but still, I felt it was a good kickoff to better days ahead.

I returned home happy, tan, surprisingly still thin after the copious amounts of prosecco and gelato, refreshed, and pretty sure that the worst had passed. I'd made it through some of my darkest days and was still standing. Whatever else was to come could never be as bad, and if so, bring it on! And then the bank started calling.

Apparently they'd been calling the whole time I was away, looking for a Seamus McVane. My mother politely told them there was no one of that name living at that address. That was when they started asking for me. *Why would they be asking for me?* I wondered.

"I don't know. They said it was a personal matter. You better call them." My mom shook her head worriedly.

So I did. The lady on the phone at the banking company was most helpful. She cleared things up for me right away.

"Yes, thank you for calling. We've been trying to get ahold of Seamus McVane regarding the CLA-Class Mercedes."

"Yes," I said tentatively. A dreadful foreboding crept over me. I was about to hear something I didn't want to hear.

"There's been some negligence on the monthly payments for the last few months," she continued pleasantly. *Oh, really?*

"I'm sorry to hear that," I said earnestly, "but you'll have to take that up with Seamus. He owns the car."

"Actually, your name appears on the title of the car as one of the owners. We've had no luck getting ahold of Mr. McVane, so that's why we've been trying to contact you."

"Wait, wait, wait, I'm still listed as an owner of the car?" I asked incredulously. Before my friend on the other line could answer, I said, "My name was supposed to be taken off and ownership transferred to Seamus almost two years ago!"

"I'm sorry, you're still listed as an owner. So if Mr. McVane can't or won't pay, we'll have to start sending the bills to you."

I think my heart might have stopped for a moment. Over my dead body was I going to start making payments. I was not going to be responsible for a car I never wanted in the first place.

"I will call Seamus and get to the bottom of this. I'm so very, very sorry. He will be making the payments, though. Thank you," I said quickly and hung up.

Damn it. I hadn't seen or talked to Seamus in months, but he would be hearing from me now. I left a couple of messages on Seamus's phone, relaying all the pertinent information (i.e., the bank was calling, he was an idiot, he'd better pay for his car, yada, yada, yada). To which he left me messages, saying there was no need to be bitchy (the nerve), he'd get around to paying the backlogged bills, and to stop bothering him with my immature phone calls. To which I responded by leaving a message saying that, like the bank, I would get off his back and stop calling once he paid his bills.

Seamus surprisingly paid his bills, and the bank stopped calling. I breathed a sigh of relief, but I knew it would be short-lived, at least until the next month came around when I'd be waiting on pins and needles to hear from the bank again. I decided it was time to get proactive and go to the car dealership to see what I could do about getting my name taken off the car title.

Bob, who'd helped us cosign for the car a few years earlier, was on vacation, so Herb helped me.

"So! You'd like to have your name taken off the car title?" he asked brightly.

"Yes," I said hopefully from the swivel chair on the other side of the desk.

"All righty then! Let me just look up the account for Seamus McVane, and we'll see what we have here!" Herb began enthusiastically pounding away at his keyboard. I waited tensely, wringing my hands.

"Okay, here we go! Ah, yes, here we are. And you are Karen, correct?" Herb looked up and smiled at me expectantly. My mouth dropped open slightly, but no words came out.

Herb looked a bit bewildered and added, "Karen ... you helped cosign for the silver S-Class Mercedes, yes?"

No. No. No.

I cleared my throat and answered with as much composure as I could, "No. I'm not Karen. I'm *Giuliana Lombardi*. Karen was Seamus's um ... last girlfriend. I cosigned for the CLA-Class."

There was a most awkward silence for a few moments as Herb mentally computed the information I'd just given him and soon realized what was going on. I noted a look of grim embarrassment, but I think it was for me. Poor Herb, how unfortunate that he'd been the one on duty to help me—*me*, a stupid fool who'd been swindled by her charlatan of an ex-boyfriend, who it appeared made a habit of getting his girlfriends to cosign expensive cars for him. I almost felt sorrier for Herb than for myself. Almost. I prayed that Herb would manage to stay his peppy, positive Polly self, because I was about to lose my shit big-time.

65

Herb now cleared his throat and said, "Okay, I see, well …"

I spoke up. "So listen, Herb, my ex-boyfriend is not making payments on time, and the bank is coming after me. Basically, I'd like my name taken off the title. Is this possible? I'm hoping you can help me with this or give me some … type of advice."

Herb looked at me and said, "Well, I guess I don't need to tell you that you should never cosign anything big like a car again for anyone, since that's financially risky." He chuckled nervously.

I was not amused. I pursed my lips and said, "Right. Anything else?"

"In all honesty, the other cosigner—in this case, your ex—would have to refinance the car in his name. If the loan you already have with the bank is in good standing and your ex has a decent, stable income, then there's a good possibility that he could get approved for a loan with the same lender. But … if he can't get a loan, then you'll really need to get the car back and sell it. Or the bank will come after you to repossess the car, and that's obviously a no-win situation for you."

I closed my eyes and pinched the bridge of my nose.

"I'm really sorry," Herb said sympathetically. "Who has the car now?"

"My ex-boyfriend."

"Do you have a set of keys to the car?" Herb asked hopefully.

"No, of course not," I answered sarcastically.

"The best you can do is to either convince your ex-boyfriend to sell the car or somehow get the car back yourself."

"Thanks." I stood up to leave.

"Good luck," Herb called as I walked away from his desk.

While I drove home like a complete automaton, my mind raced with the clarity of it all. Everything now made sense. Seamus had played the love game with me and had ingratiated himself with my family until he'd been able to get me to cosign the lease. It was shortly after he'd gotten the Mercedes that things had begun to really fall apart, with the avoidance of my family, my friends, and me.

Let's face it, I'd been charmed by a con artist, a total sociopath. Perhaps, without the Irish accent, I wouldn't have been as taken in, I tried to convince myself. But, no, I reasoned, Seamus had just been very, very good at hiding whom he really was. And since I really wasn't a member of the close-knit Irish community, I'd received no friendly warnings as to his less-than-stellar reputation. God, I'd been the perfect victim.

Still, I berated myself mercilessly. *How stupid could you be? But I loved him,* I whimpered back to myself. *He never loved you! But I thought he had … once. You just wasted three years of your life,* I countered back. I couldn't argue with myself on that one.

And then I got angry. My next call to Seamus—well, I'll spare you the exact conversation, as it included a plethora of very unladylike expletives. In fact, to this day, I have no idea where they all came from. But I was in a rage, and there was a lot of hysterical ranting about my knowing what he'd done and how he'd better pay or sell the car.

In turn, Seamus did his fair share of swearing at me and said there was no way he was going to sell the car and to leave him alone. I hung up on him in the middle of his screaming. It was all very Jerry Springer–like, I'm embarrassed to admit.

A month later, when the bank began calling me again, I wasn't surprised. And I was ready to step it up and do something more than leave bitchy messages on Seamus's phone, because that obviously wasn't working. I made a call to a parent whose two children I had taught a few years back. The parent was a lawyer. My questions for him were basically: Did I need to get legal help? Was this something I should pursue?

Brian Riley listened while I sheepishly told him about the cosigning of the car, etc. I waited for him to tut-tut and tell me what an idiot I was, because, well, I was. Instead, he said, "This guy's a real asshole. *Nobody* does that to Giuliana Lombardi and gets away with it. I'm gonna help you with this."

"Really?" I said, relieved that there was actually somebody who could possibly help me.

"You bet. Listen, possession is nine-tenths of the law. You need to get the car back before the bank repossesses it. Is there a way for you to do that?"

"I think so, but I'd need to make a few calls first," I said hesitantly. I'd have to get the number of the English guy, Ian, whom Seamus now lived with. He worked with my sister's boyfriend, Brendan, so it wouldn't be too hard to get ahold of him. But would Ian be willing to help me?

I didn't know, but I was banking on him being one of the many who couldn't stand Seamus.

Brian said, "Okay, good. Make your calls, see if there's a way to get the car, and call me back. Then we'll take it from there."

"Okay, thanks so much, Brian. I really appreciate it," I said, feeling my eyes tear up.

"Absolutely. This'll be child's play. He's not going to get away with this. Jesus, he's giving us Irish a bad name!"

Later that day, I dialed Ian's phone and held my breath. I knew Ian as an acquaintance, but I had no idea what he'd say. As luck would have it, I needn't have been worried. After explaining myself and my need to get the car, Ian said, "I'll tell you, Giuliana, I may live with him, but I don't like him. I don't like how he treated you, and I don't like how he treats women." He continued cryptically, "So, *let's just say*, Seamus leaves his Mercedes in the garage and takes his truck to work." Seamus had a truck now? I wondered if the Irish store girlfriend had helped make that possible.

Ian continued conspiratorially, "And let's just say the side door to the house will be unlocked. Let's also just say that Seamus always leaves his keys on the dining room table. But you did not hear this from me. You get what I mean?"

"Perfectly," I answered.

"Okay, then, just let me know when this covert operation is going to happen so I can make sure everything's where it's supposed to be."

"Thanks, Ian."

"Cheers."

The next day I spoke to *my attorney* (I still get a thrill out of saying that). Brian was quite ecstatic with my news of being able to get the car.

"Great! How soon can you go get it? Tomorrow?"

"Uh, okay. I just have to make sure I have coverage in my classroom," I said, wincing. My principal was of the old-school teaching ilk—as in, it didn't matter what state you were in (you could have one foot in the grave), but you'd better not call in sick. It was safe to say that if I came to school with the likes of tuberculosis, hacking up a lung or two, she would most likely hand me a couple of throat lozenges and tell me to get back to work. Therefore, I wasn't quite sure if she'd be up for letting me leave for an hour or so to "steal" my car back. Well, she was going to have to be. I had to get to the car while Seamus was at work.

"Also, there's just one other thing," I said. "I can't drive a stick shift." Why had I never learned how to drive a stick shift? Seamus had actually tried to teach me. He'd said that since the car was half mine I should be able to drive it. Funny, huh? One lesson was enough for me to know I'd never get it, and I was fine with that. I had no patience. Clearly, I already knew how to drive. Why would I forego the smooth ease of an automatic for nonstop potential stalling and grinding of gears? I didn't even want to think about what might happen should I come to a stop sign at the top of a hill. It just wasn't happening. I think it's safe to say that Seamus didn't have much patience trying to teach me either. Had I known that one day I'd need to drive that car away, à la a *Charlie's Angels* episode, I would've tried a little harder. Oh, the bitter irony of it all.

Brian eased my fears. "Don't worry. I'll send my assistant, Jamie, over tomorrow. She'll go with you and can drive the car back to my work. We have a private garage, and we'll keep it safe there. What you need to do when you get there is check the trunk and the glove compartment and take out everything that's his and leave it there. And you're going to leave a note for him. Do you have a pen and paper?"

"Uh, yeah," I said, scrambling to find something to write on.

"Okay, write this down." Brian began dictating.

I scribbled it all down furiously.

"All right, now don't worry about anything. I'll send Jamie over tomorrow around your recess time, and then we'll talk after it's all been done."

Don't worry? I'd try not to, but there were a lot of what-ifs. What if Seamus was sick tomorrow and didn't go to work? What if he decided to come home to get something while we were there? What if Ian had been lying to me and told Seamus what I was up to? What if somebody saw us and called the cops? Technically, I wasn't doing anything illegal. I was not breaking and entering. And I wasn't stealing either. I was simply taking something back that actually belonged to me. I had to do this. Seamus had gotten away with quite a bit of shit. He had screwed me over, but I would not let his dishonesty take me down financially. He'd brought this on himself. I'd had enough. I was a nice person, but

69

let it be known, I wasn't a pathetic doormat. Operation Mercedes CLA-Class was on.

Everything was a go. When I explained to my principal the car situation and why it was imperative that I had to go during school hours, she immediately said no problem and she'd cover for me herself. *Wow*. Jamie showed up on time, and we drove the ten minutes to the address. The street was quiet, and we parked a couple of houses away. I prayed that Ian had remembered to leave the side door unlocked. In general, well, I prayed. *Let everything go smoothly. Please.*

We went in through the side gate, and the door was unlocked. The car keys were sitting in the middle of the dining room table, where Ian said they'd be. We made a quick sweep through the car and left Seamus's CDs and golf clubs on the garage floor.

"Did you leave the note on the table?" Jamie reminded me.

Ah, yes, the note. The pièce de résistance. It read:

Seamus,

I have received a default notice from the bank regarding the car. I cannot have the bank repossess the car and be subjected to all the charges and the low value I will get on resale. I intend to sell the car and pay off the loan. If you have any questions regarding this, contact my attorney, Brian Riley, at the above number.

Giuliana

I'd really wanted to add my own finishing touches, such as "And by the way, thanks for nothing, you asshole!" or "Karma's a bitch, dickhead! Sucks to be you!" But I thought, perhaps, that might be adding fuel to the fire. As it stood, Seamus would be absolutely livid. He was sure to go ballistic, and I'd no doubt be hearing from him soon. I smiled and left the note on the table.

Jamie backed the car out of the garage. I closed the garage and went out the side door. It was done. I had done it. I watched the black

Mercedes, a symbol of my misery and anger, drive away. I got in my car and headed back to school.

I was right. To say Seamus was infuriated was putting it a tad mildly. He left several irate messages on my phone that evening, demanding to know where the car was, how I'd gotten in, and that he was going to call the police. But I'd also talked to Brian that evening and knew that he'd already heard from Seamus and had told him that he didn't have a leg to stand on by going to the police. I also had a few phone chats with Ian, who was a bit worried.

"He's all over me, asking if I let you in. I denied it, but make sure this doesn't get out. I know everyone hates the bastard, but I don't want to be known about town as a snitch."

I was fairly sure people would be lining up to buy Ian drinks, but I promised, "Don't worry, your name will never be mentioned. You have my word." *Jeez!* But my phone was blowing up with the calls, and a lot of them were from my close girlfriends, who were all very congratulatory. It was Team Giuliana all the way.

A couple of days later, I finally took one of Seamus's calls.

"Hello?" I said cavalierly. I waited for the tirade to begin, and it did.

"I want to know where the hell the car is!" he screamed.

When I didn't answer, Seamus continued his shrieking. "I want to know who fucking let you in!"

"Nobody let me in," I answered simply.

"Well, then I'm gonna call the police and have you arrested for breaking in!" he shouted.

I rolled my eyes. "I didn't break in. The side door was unlocked."

Ignoring my reply, Seamus shouted once again, "I want to know who let you in! Was it Ian?"

"I walked in, Seamus! You should really lock your side door. Ian has nothing to do with this."

"You're a fucking liar! I can have you arrested!" he screamed.

Now I was starting to get annoyed. "*I'm a liar*, really? *Arrested*, really? I don't think so. If you have anything else to say, call my lawyer." I hung up on him smugly.

Seamus had a lot more to say, but I let Brian Riley handle it. I never spoke to Seamus or saw him again. About six months later Brian Riley called me with an update on the car, which had since been sitting at the dealership. Apparently, Seamus had pleaded and gotten the dealership to release the car back to him on the promise that he'd make good on all his monthly payments. There was not much I could do but wait and see.

Summer came around, and I left on another trip to Italy with friends. I returned to find that once again, the bank was calling me about the Mercedes. I made a quick call to Brian and was told to get ahold of the car again, before the bank did. I had no idea where Seamus was living now. He'd moved several times. I questioned Irish Norm, but even he wasn't sure of Seamus's living quarters.

"All I know, Giuliana, is that I've heard he lives in some apartment behind the high school Sunnybrae." He shook his head.

Great, there were a zillion apartment buildings behind the high school. This wouldn't be a problem if Seamus was actually around and I could get one of the Irish folk to contact him. But, no, the word was that he'd left the country suddenly to go back to Tyrone. No wonder the bank hadn't received any payments.

Jane (yes, Jane, my friend of the night I met Seamus) accompanied me on this mission. At least I didn't have to worry about Seamus showing up and foiling my plan to get the car.

We drove slowly down the street behind the high school. And lo and behold, there was the CLA-Class, the bane of my existence (aside from Seamus), parked on the street in front of one of the apartment buildings.

"There it is!" I shouted.

The car had apparently been sitting there for a while. It was dirty and had numerous flyers stuck under its windshield wipers.

Jane and I walked up to the apartment building and saw that Seamus McVane was noted on the list of residents.

"Apartment 101. Let's see if we can get in and find the keys," Jane cried excitedly. "I feel like we're Cagney and Lacey or something!"

And just like that, someone exited the building and we scooted in. We walked down the hallway, peering at each door. Up ahead, there was a door that had yellow caution tape across it. As we got closer we saw that it was apartment 101.

"Oh my God," murmured Jane.

A notice had been tacked to the door. I looked at Jane and then turned and read it out loud.

"Notice: Seamus McVane has hereby been evicted due to repeated failure to pay rent. Holy crap. Are we surprised?" I asked Jane.

She shook her head and said, "Let's go in."

"We can't go in! It's going to be locked anyway!" I hissed, looking up and down the hallway nervously.

Ignoring me, Jane tugged her sweatshirt down over her hand (lest we leave any incriminating fingerprints) and turned the doorknob. *Presto!* The door opened. I stared at her in disbelief.

"Well, come on!" she whispered. "Before someone sees us!"

We shimmied under the yellow tape and quickly closed the door behind us. The place was in total and utter disarray. It seemed the evictee had left in quite a hurry. Hefty bags full of clothing lined the walls, there were papers strewn all over the table, and cartons of disgusting old Chinese food were left opened on the kitchen counter. Minus the body, it looked like something out of a *CSI* episode.

Jane wrinkled her nose and said, "Wanna look around? Anything in here that might belong to you that you want?"

I thought about all that expensive Pottery Barn bedding I'd bought Seamus. And the photo albums I'd made him. And the DVD collector's edition of James Bond films that my mom had thoughtfully bought him one Christmas. Yeah, I thought of a lot of things.

"No, I don't want anything. Just the car keys," I answered quietly. I turned and looked at the counter again, and there were the keys to the Mercedes, in plain sight. I picked them up and jingled them in front of Jane.

"Jesus, do you think he knew you'd be coming for these?" she asked in disbelief.

"I don't know, but let's get out of here."

The car sat in my driveway for quite some time while prospective buyers came every once in a blue moon to check it out. Most of them were Asian teenagers who wanted a fast car, but they weren't willing or able to pay the asking price. You know, the price that I would have to pay the bank off with. Bob (and poor Herb too) felt sorry for me and let the car sit at the dealership for a few months, but no one was interested.

It finally went to auction and sold for twelve thousand dollars. Eight thousand dollars less than what was owed on it, but it was finally gone.

I hear stories about Seamus every once in a while. Just as I've completely forgotten about his existence, I'll run into someone in a one of the local Irish bars and be reminded with the old "Jesus, but I hated him! Aw, sure, you were too good for him!" Sometimes I get a Seamus "sighting" report. "I heard he was seen in the city. Somehow, living in the Marina!"

I shrug blandly and say, "Really? I have no idea what he's up to."

And every once in a while, I still get this: "Ah, you're the one that stole the car from McVane! Fair play to ya! I'd like to shake yer hand. Well done, well done!"

I smile demurely and say, "I didn't steal it. I just took back what was mine."

My Own Personal Jesus

So you'd assume after all the drama with Seamus, I'd be done with and altogether avoid anything of the Irish nature—as in Irish bars, Irish people, and possibly even potatoes. And aside from my Irish friend, Josie, and the odd potato every once in a while, you've assumed correctly—it wasn't that Seamus had tarnished my view of the Irish. On the contrary, I just couldn't find it in me to *not* like the Irish. I mean, how can you? I knew Seamus was the exception to the Irish rule, or specifically to all mankind. It really wasn't an "Irish" situation but rather an unfortunately I-dated-an-asshole incident.

Yet while I realized that, I still felt the need to shun all Irishness for quite some time. Because of the immense shame and total embarrassment I felt by Seamus completely duping me, I developed a bit of a paranoid attitude. *I've been made to look a fool.* Everywhere I went, I felt as if the Irish were watching and sniggering behind their hands.

"Hey, Paddy, need a car? I hear Giuliana's good for one of those! Pathetic, isn't she?"

Yes, I obsessed nonstop about people thinking I was a stupid fool. I was obsessed particularly with the Irish thinking I was a stupid fool (as if they didn't have anything better to talk about). But this was my bad breakup, and it was all about me. To say I was emotionally fragile was an understatement. My friends, emotionally worn out themselves from having to act as my round-the-clock grief counselors/cheerleaders, finally had an intervention with me and persuaded me to seek therapy and preferably not from them. I can't say I blamed them. I was a mess.

Enter my (short-lived) real therapist, Susan. Boy, did she have her work cut out for her. Before you go crediting all my emotional baggage to Seamus, you should know I had a whole host of other issues going on.

Take my mother, who had almost died that year due to complications from diabetes, or my binge eating and drinking, which were problematic, to say the least. My weight was constantly yo-yoing. My closet housed four different sizes of clothes to accommodate my weight fluctuations. Or take my shopping. I'd always been an excellent shopper, if I have to brag about something. But the shopping took a turn for the excessive (I have a penchant for very expensive clothes), which is all good and fine if you're one of the Kardashians, not if you're a Catholic schoolteacher who makes a pittance. Pair that with the money I'd lost on the Mercedes, and debt was starting to become an issue, one that I didn't want to acknowledge.

Seamus, the worst of my troubles? Ha! He was just the tip of the iceberg. I felt myself spiraling downward and fast. It seemed I had lost all control in my life. And my moods swung from very happy and social (while drinking) to sullen and depressed (while drinking or not). I cried at the drop of a hat over nothing or anything, and I couldn't stop. If I didn't have to work, I would've stayed in bed and slept away a couple of years. "Depression, thy name is Giuliana" was my calling card.

So when my friends tearfully suggested therapy, let's just say I was receptive. I mean, it couldn't make me feel worse than I already did, could it? So, back to Susan, my therapist. With me, Susan had a lot to work with. Despite this, somehow the sessions always ended up with her getting me to talk about Seamus. My shoulders would automatically hunch, and my throat would feel tight as I talked about him. My voice would rise with uncontrollable anger.

And then anger would give way to a flood of tears, something akin to Niagara Falls, I'd say. Damn that Susan, but she could always get me to cry, although, at that point of my life, it wasn't a difficult thing. However, I always felt like I was on a Barbara Walters special. I'd go in mentally rehearsing, "You will *not* cry today! Be strong! There will be no tears! She is not going to get you to cry. Do you hear me?" But she always did. I just couldn't help it. I was a wreck. If I wasn't mad, I was sad. If I wasn't sad, I was frightened and worried. My judgment in men had been so off, so wrong. How could I trust myself again? What if I got taken in by another charming/evil swindler?

Susan would reason with me, "Giuliana, if you had a friend or a sister that this had happened to, what would you say to her?"

"This wouldn't happen to any of my friends or my sister, since they're not *stupid* like me!" I'd sputter vehemently before grabbing another Kleenex and blubbering into it.

Susan, being ever the calm professional, would ignore my outburst and reply again, "What would you say to a friend? Come on now, what would you say?"

I'd sniffle and dab at my once-again leaking eyes. "I'd tell her it wasn't her fault. She didn't know any better."

"That's right, Giuliana! *You* didn't know any better. It wasn't *your* fault."

"But what if it happens again with someone else?" I cried.

"It won't happen again, because now you know what to look for. You look at a man's friends. Does he have any? What are they like?"

I sniffled in agreement. Yeah, the fact that Seamus had just about no friends should've been a big tip-off, I supposed. Susan continued, "Does he have a job? Where does he live? Does he move around a lot?"

I winced, remembering that I had thought it odd that Seamus had moved at least four different times while we'd been dating, no doubt because he'd owed people money, wasn't paying rent on time, or was possibly a fugitive of the law somewhere. But at the time I'd never thought to question it.

"Does he try to get too involved with you too soon?" I winced again. I had ignored my gut instinct so many times.

"Listen to yourself. You are an honest person, but not everyone else is. So if it doesn't feel right, it's probably because it isn't," Susan added, thus condoning my thoughts on the matter.

"Okay," I said, none too convincingly, and honked my nose again into my soggy hankie.

"Good! Now for our next session, I'd like you to start thinking about your overshopping. We'll start with that," Susan said brightly.

"Okay," I said, collecting all my wadded-up tissues. I knew better, though. We weren't going to talk about my shopping next time. I wasn't going back. I'd done my three months of therapy and only felt slightly better about myself. Yes, yes, in hindsight I know that therapy is an ongoing process that does not follow a specific time frame. At that point though, I was so damn tired of crying all the time. I cried enough at home, and when I was out with friends, and when I was in my car, and in my classroom too, when the kids were out at recess, of course. You get the picture. I didn't need to pay money for a full hour of balling my eyes out. I always left feeling drained and depleted of all energy. Shouldn't I be feeling better at the end of each session?

In essence, I felt I'd gotten enough out of the sessions. Basically after all our discussions, it came down to these things: my mom needed to take better care of herself (she had her own issues), Seamus was a jerk who'd taken advantage of my trusting nature, I now knew the red flags to look for with men and not to ignore them, I was self-medicating with binge eating and drinking, I had a shopping problem (also a form of some kind of screwed-up self-medicating or overcompensating for a lack of self-esteem), etc. Yep, I knew what was wrong with me. I didn't need to pay to have somebody tell me my issues, and I certainly didn't want to cry over them anymore. It was time to move on, and I'd do it my own way.

It was during the Susan era that I became friends with Maggie. Maggie was part of the Irish community. Her parents, like so many others in the sixties and seventies, had emigrated to the San Francisco Bay Area, gotten married, and started a family. Having a strong Irish background, it was only natural that Maggie would frequent the local Irish bars and that our paths would eventually cross.

While dating Seamus, I'd met her a few times at O'Hooley's. Maggie would be there with Ryan, her Irish boyfriend from Waterford. While Seamus talked to Irish people (and not me), Maggie, noticing me sitting off to the side, would always make a point to say hi and stop to chat.

And believe me, Maggie could've ignored me. She had special membership in the Irish ladies' club. While she was born in the States, her parents were Irish, and therefore, she was a part of the group. I was just an outsider. Aside from a "Hello" every now and then, the Irish ladies walked past and huddled together in one corner of the bar. I sat and nursed my drinks by myself. Therefore, I was always appreciative of Maggie's friendliness. I felt there was some sort of camaraderie, two

American girls with Irish boyfriends bonding. Or she might've just felt sorry for me.

Anyway, sometime after the implosion of my relationship with Seamus and the Mercedes heist, I stumbled into the upscale clothing boutique in Burlington in which Maggie worked. I remembered she'd told me she worked there, but the clothes always seemed so intimidatingly chic and expensive (yes, even for me), so I'd never gone in. However, I'd always thought Maggie was lovely, and just because Seamus was a loser didn't mean I should be barred from one day having my own lot of Irish friends. Perhaps there was a chance that not all Irish people thought I was a total moron.

As it turns out, Maggie didn't think I was a moron. "Ugh, I never liked that guy! Oh, I just can't stand him!"

Yes, well, I was used to that standard response from people.

Then she added, shaking her head in bewilderment, "I always wondered why such a nice girl like you was dating him."

I'd been wondering that same thing about myself. It was refreshing to hear somebody else utter it out loud, though. Suffice it to say, she and I became fast friends. I also became very good friends with the clothing in the boutique, but that's another story altogether.

Anyway, hanging out with Maggie and her boyfriend, I was slowly drawn back into the Irish social scene. Ah, how I'd missed it. My self-imposed quarantine was over. I was back. Hopefully nobody would hold my relationship with Seamus against me. Hell, hopefully they wouldn't even remember me. And luckily I wouldn't be running into Seamus, since he was back in Ireland. Yes, all conditions were right for my reinitiation into Irish (night) life.

And just so you know, I wasn't looking to meet and date anyone Irish. I wasn't looking to date anyone at all really. I was quite skeptical of having a relationship, especially one that could potentially involve me being bamboozled into buying some sort of sporty transportation. While I knew what I was supposed to be on the lookout for regarding men and bad behavior, I was still highly distraught about my ability to make sound decisions.

Therefore, I decided to keep my social life light and breezy. There would be no romance. Oh, no-ho-ho, sir! I was just out to have some fun, and I pushed all those worrisome relationship thoughts to the back of my mind. I was going to make sure that making bad decisions regarding my love life was going to be a nonissue, since I was going to make a point to keep my love life pretty much nonexistent. I wasn't out looking for anyone; therefore, I would not be putting myself out there to possibly get hurt. It seemed like a logical thought process. So I thought.

And in the process of not looking for anyone in particular, I met Finn O'Connell. Well, I'd met him before, a couple of years earlier when I was dating Seamus, but he was just "Young Finn." Young Finn, so as not to be confused, God forbid, with the *one* other Finn in the pub scene. I didn't think it was likely to happen, since the two looked nothing alike. Young Finn was good-looking and, for lack of a better word, young. Well, he was twenty-one. The other Finn was old and not good-looking. He was probably my age (a whopping thirty-one) but looked like he was ten to fifteen years older.

Therefore, the likelihood of the two of them ever being mistaken for each other was borderline impossible. However, it seemed everyone in the bar had a nickname. I am lucky to have escaped over the years without one (that I know of). But of course, thankfully, I have never considered or treated O'Hooley's like my second home.

Everyone had a nickname, and everyone had a story of some sort. Finn was rumored to have an on-again/off-again drug problem. And as bar gossip would have it, he was always getting shipped off by his family to different rehabs. After the rehab stints were up, he'd once again eventually show up in the Irish bars—for the better or worse, one never knew (that is, until he fell back off the wagon, and then you knew).

Of course, this was all only hearsay to me. I knew him not. Aside from being reintroduced to each other every so often (I was forever being reintroduced to people in the bars probably due to everyone's alcohol-induced amnesia), Finn was just one of the Irish cast of characters I vaguely knew. I had no reason to think much else about him. He was not what I would call in my age bracket, and I had a boyfriend to boot. So that was that.

Three and a half years later, it was a crowded night in O'Hooley's. It was the night before Easter, and everyone was out. Around here, it's a given that the night before a big holiday you must go out and you must drink a lot … and have a heinous hangover the next day, but that's all right because it's a holiday and you don't have to work. Well, that was the general mentality—the rule, if you will. As we get older (and some of us wiser), we may choose to ignore the rule and stay home, out of a sense of responsibility or duty to spouses, children, the turkey or leg of lamb we're supposed to be preparing, whatever. And then we can feel smug and satisfied the next morning when we don't have rotten hangovers like everyone else. The rest of us, though, will spend half the day napping on the couch and will just be coming to by the time the aforementioned turkey or leg of lamb is ready. It just happens.

Like I said, it was the night before Easter. Maggie and I were meeting her boyfriend, Ryan, and his friends at O'Hooley's. One of his friends Maggie just positively gushed about. I'd known Maggie only a short time, but if there was one thing I'd figured out about her, it was that she was not, by nature, a gusher. Direct and no-nonsense, she was. Overly exaggerating and sycophantic, she definitely was not. You knew where you stood with Maggie, and that was fine by me. Therefore, when she went on and on about this friend of Ryan's, and in an almost schoolgirly type way, I couldn't help but listen in amusement while wondering if she might even have a slight crush on the guy.

"I totally have a crush on him. You know what I mean. I just love him. He's so damn hot. And he's such a sweetie. Just a really sweet guy." Maggie sighed.

Wow, compliments and now she was sighing too? I wondered who this magical Irish guy was.

"It's Finn O'Connell," she said, as if reading my mind. Seeing a look of alarm pass over my face, Maggie quickly said, "Young Finn, not the other one."

"Oh, that one," I said. "Did he just have a kid or something?"

Maggie scowled and said harshly, "Yes, he now has a baby with that crazy bitch, Lydia. Ugh, can't stand her!"

She sighed again, but this time sadly. I was all ears. I loved getting the dirt, like any other Irish (or not) person.

"The baby is adorable, but Lydia and Finn, together … a mess. He's no saint, and we all know that, but I blame her for a lot of his issues." Maggie continued, "When they were together, it was a nightmare.

Hopefully with the baby, that'll change, but she's crazy. Finn needs to get away from her."

Yikes. I felt sorry for the poor guy. Little did I know I'd become his confessor and confidante that entire evening. After being re-reintroduced to Finn, Maggie and I ended up snagging bar stools next to Finn. Apparently, he'd long beaten the crowds for his bar stool. I sat in the middle of Finn and Maggie. As Ryan and Maggie caught up with Finn, I found myself taking Finn in—not checking him out, per se, but really looking at him. It was eerie, but for some reason he reminded me of someone. Someone, *someone.* Who was it? I puzzled silently while knocking back some vodka sodas. He had steely blue eyes offset by a somewhat tan (and therefore very un-Irish) complexion. His head was shaved, and his sparse goatee was a blondish light brown. He had nice lips and a good set of teeth, but even at twenty-three they were starting to yellow just a tinge from his chain-smoking.

And I couldn't tell you what he was wearing, which is quite uncharacteristic of me. I remember what I've worn to every major event in my life starting with picture day in kindergarten. And I will remember what everyone else is wearing too. I'm special like that or else just very shallow and clothing-obsessed. Take your pick. But I don't for the life of me remember what Finn was wearing. I was simply too fixated on figuring out who he reminded me of.

And then without warning, he began talking to me. "Hello, Giuliana, how are ya?" He had a soft accent, not heavy like a lot of the others. He and his family had moved to the States when he was eleven. The accent was slight, but it was there. I loved it.

"Congratulations on the new baby!" I said, not sure how long I'd be able to carry on a conversation with Finn, ten years younger than me, a supposed druggie, etc. Well, we didn't have a lot in common, you know? And Maggie was right. He was beautiful, in a rugged and brooding way. It was downright disconcerting how cute he was. Not that I was thinking that at all.

However, I fretted about conversational topics for nothing. You see, I'd uttered the magic words "new baby." That was all it took. All brand-spanking-new parents are the same when asked about the baby. It doesn't matter how sleep-deprived or, in this case, slightly intoxicated they are. They immediately and enthusiastically want to tell you all about their bundle of joy. It's a universal parental thing. Finn was no different. And I was glad. He positively glowed in the dingy low light of O'Hooley's. Let me tell you that's not an easy feat either.

"Aw, thank you, Giuliana. She's great, just great." And before I knew it, the wallet was whipped out, and I was being shown an assortment of baby pics. It was all very, very sweet. Aside from his youth and his personal issues (which I'd yet to hear in full detail), Finn was a normal (so to speak) father who adored his new baby.

And seeing as how babies have to come from somewhere, as in there must have been a mother involved somehow, the conversation turned to Finn's baby mama, the ill-spoken-of Lydia. He loved her—oh, he did—or so he claimed. But all they did was fight, and he couldn't stand her. They just didn't get along at all. But he loved her.

And back and forth Finn went. I was certainly not one to talk, but it seemed an ill-fated match to me. I sipped away at my vodka soda while nodding and *hmm-ing* in the appropriate places. Clearly, I had no expertise to offer on such matters. What could he do? If Finn wanted to be a part of his daughter's life, he was forever going to have to deal with Lydia. However, marrying her, as he'd suggested he was thinking of, didn't seem the proper solution. I wanted to scream, "No! What are you thinking? Don't do it!" But I didn't. I gathered that Finn really wasn't asking for my advice. It was more of an alcohol-spurred venting session, and I was the particular recipient of the moment. For the record though, I am an excellent listener, especially to other people's sob stories. I admit I do love hearing about others' problems. I suppose it's a combination of morbid curiosity about others, as well as making me feel like I'm not the only dysfunctional loser on the planet.

And I certainly did not mind acting as Finn's faux therapist. It gave me an excuse to purposely stare at him. Well, it would've been rude of me not to. And in the process of listening to Finn and looking at him, it dawned on me whom he looked like. Jesus. As in Christ. Not that I have ever seen Jesus in the flesh, but all I could think about was the bulletin board in my childhood bedroom, say circa second or third grade. Being of the Catholic persuasion and having gone to a Catholic school that was run by nuns made for a pretty holy childhood. I mean, I know I wasn't the only girl in my class who idolized our teacher, Sr. Benedetta, and wanted to become a nun as soon as I received my First Communion.

My bulletin board had become a mecca of juxtapositional features: the secular likes of Andy Gibb, Olivia Newton John, the 49ers team picture, and so on, were on one side, and the other half had become a shrine to the Virgin Mary, covered with various holy cards I'd received for my First Communion. And let's not forget Mary's son, the Big J. C. He took up a good portion of that bulletin board real estate. Smack in the middle of the Mary holy cards was the traditional picture of the Sacred Heart of Jesus. If you're any kind of Catholic, you know the picture: Dreamy-looking Jesus, halo outlining light-brown shoulder-length hair, blue eyes, full lips, goatee, His sacred heart ensconced in a crown of thorns, and dripping blood. It is the quintessential Jesus picture that all old-school Catholics had either hanging in their home or tucked away in their wallets (or on their second-grade bulletin board). In all goobery honesty, when you're very young and very Catholic, Mary and Jesus are complete superstars. If there'd been a T-shirt back then that read on one side *Who's Yo Mama? Mary* and on the other side *Jesus Is My Homeboy*, it's certain I would've been sporting it to the roller rink and all around town.

So it had been Jesus all along. It was odd, yet … well, it was just odd—kind of like when you go to a party and you're drawn toward someone and you just can't put your finger on it, but they seem so familiar to you. And then you find out that someone is really a long-lost cousin thrice removed whom you've never met but who looks strikingly like your aunt Bea. Or he could look like Jesus.

I suppose the vodka sodas could've played a small part in this weird religious doppelgänger, but just to be sure, I turned toward Maggie to ask her opinion. Before I could, she said with a wink, "Well, Finn's certainly taken a liking to you. What have you two been talking about for so long?"

I waved her off, saying, "Oh, nothing. He's just been telling me the saga of Lydia."

Maggie rolled her eyes and said, "Well, try convincing him to stay away from her!"

"Yeah, well, I'm pretty sure he wants to marry her." I shrugged.

Maggie visibly shuddered and said, "And that's about the worst idea ever. Somebody needs to knock some sense into him. He just doesn't listen to anyone."

"Right," I said. It was all out of my hands, and he still looked like Jesus with short hair, which was of utmost importance to me at that moment. I glanced at Finn sideways and whispered behind my hand to Maggie, "Is it me, but Finn looks like Jesus, doesn't he?"

She cocked her head to the side and said, "Huh. Yeah, he does. Weird. Only you would notice that!" She shook her head and laughed.

Finn suddenly thumped his beer bottle down on the bar and shouted at us, "What are you talking about?"

"Uh, nothing," I lied.

"I know you're talking about me. What are you saying?" he nearly screamed. I assumed some sort of drug-related paranoia had taken hold of him and was the cause of this outburst.

I sheepishly said, "I uh, just said, uh … you kinda look like … Jesus." I hoped he didn't take his beer bottle and smash it over my head. I mean, it was a compliment. I waited, and I admit I was a bit scared.

He looked at me for a few moments and then answered, "Oh. Okay," and turned back to his beer.

I exhaled and looked at Maggie, who was chuckling at my frightened expense.

"What? That was scary," I said.

"Please, Finn wouldn't hurt a fly." Maggie took a sip of her cider.

"Is he … okay now?" I asked. I definitely didn't think it was a good idea to piss off someone who might potentially be on drugs. I'd seen one too many of those ABC after-school specials in my day.

"Don't really know. Ryan says he's been fine. Supposedly. It's just the drinking he needs to worry about."

I looked at Maggie quizzically. She answered matter-of-factly, "Finn's got a drinking problem."

Wow. I'd only heard about the drugs. Alcoholic too? *What is he doing in a bar?* Oh, wait, he had a problem with the drink (as they all said). *That's* what he was doing in a bar. But I couldn't help but wonder why his friends stood by and watched him drink like it was no big deal.

Didn't anyone care? Of course, if I only knew then what I know now about people with drinking problems, I would've understood.

I guess Maggie sensed my confusion. She said, "There's nothing anyone can really say to Finn. Everyone has tried to have interventions with him. It doesn't matter, because in the end, he's going to do what he wants to do. There's no telling him anything."

"Sad" was all I could think to comment.

"I know," said Maggie, shrugging in resignation.

"But doesn't it bother you guys seeing him here drinking?" I asked incredulously.

"Of course, but if anyone said anything, he'd just go find somewhere else to drink. Although lately his drinking doesn't seem too out of hand. He hasn't gotten too crazy, and I've seen him really fucked up. As long as nothing sets him off, like that bitch, Lydia. Then he usually falls off the wagon big-time and back into drugs."

We both sat and watched Finn as he waved the barmaid over for another beer.

"And a round for the girls and Ryan too, thanks," he said and nodded at us before turning to talk to the drunken patron next to him.

Maggie sighed and shook her head. "Yep, he got all the looks and *all* the problems."

At the end of the evening, which was really two in the morning, we all stood outside the bar, waiting for cabs. An empty cab pulled up, and Ryan said, "You take it, Giuliana," as we were all going in different directions.

"Night!" I waved over my shoulder as I opened the cab door.

That's when I heard Finn say to Ryan and Maggie, "I'm going with Giuliana." I turned and looked back. *What?* I thought.

"No, he's not. Tell him he's not, Ryan," Maggie stated.

Ryan shrugged at her, and Maggie called out, "Leave Giuliana alone, Finn."

I decided it was best to get into the cab. As I did, Maggie shouted at Finn, "Finn, she doesn't need any more drama!"

Before the cab could pull away, Finn had hopped in and slid next to me in the backseat. We stared at each other for a moment, and then Finn said earnestly, "Giuliana, I'm going home with you."

Uh, no he was not, especially since I was sleeping over at my grandmother's house that night. Since my parents had divorced when I was six, it had become a family tradition for Mom, Annie, and me to sleep overnight at my grandparents' house the nights before Christmas and Easter. And, no, it didn't matter that I was still doing so at thirty-three. The only reason my sister wasn't was that she'd just gotten married. Flimsy excuse though, I thought. However, I hardly thought Finn should be my sister's backup.

"No, you're not coming home with me," I stated firmly.

"I am," he said just as firmly.

"Sorry, *no*," I said, noticing the cab driver eyeing us in the rearview mirror.

"Where to, miss?" he asked.

"Turn north on El Dorado, and I'll tell you where to go from there."

"What about him?" the cabbie asked while pulling away from the curb. I turned back to see Maggie shaking her head and, it looked like, yelling at Ryan.

I answered quickly, "He's going home, to *his* home. Where do you live, Finn?"

"Burlington, but I'm not going there. I'm coming home with you." He pouted, as if this was something that was actually going to happen. I had no idea what was going on, but he was not coming to Grandma's with me.

"Look," I began, "I'm going to my grandma's house." I assumed that would make any sort of normal fellow hop out of the cab while it was still moving.

"I don't care. I'm going home with you," Finn said obstinately. Oh, yeah, I'd forgotten Finn wasn't normal. Maggie was right. There was no telling him anything. Visions of my eighty-five-year-old grandmother finding (and smelling) an alcohol-pickled Finn asleep on the living room couch in, oh, say, four hours flashed through my mind.

"Stop the cab. Here's my car! Thanks so much!" I threw a five at the cabbie and climbed out. Finn clambered out after me. I figured he would. Since he was insistent on coming with me to Grandma's, my new plan was to drive him home, thus forcing him to have to get out of my car, which was when I would drive away quickly. Never mind that

I shouldn't have been driving at all. I had a crisis on my hands, and he needed to be dropped off at his home.

"You're going to have to tell me how to get to your place," I said as I backed out of the corner parking lot on the avenue.

"Okay," he said quietly. A few minutes later, I pulled up in front of his darkened house. I sincerely hoped I wasn't going to have to argue with Finn about his getting out of the car.

"Well, have a nice Easter," I said brightly. *Why does he have to be so cute?* It was too bad that he was ten years younger. And had a drug problem. And was an alcoholic. And had a new baby with a girl who'd probably kill me if she knew I'd driven her baby daddy home. Right, the relationship between the two of us was doomed from the get-go. However, there was no relationship in sight, so I was safe.

He looked at me a moment, with slightly droopy eyes, and then said, "Okay, thanks. You too."

I thought I was off the hook, but Finn turned toward me sharply and leaned in to kiss me. I jerked my head back.

"What's wrong?" Finn asked.

"Finn, look, you're a doll, but you just spent the whole night telling me how much you love Lydia. I just … can't. I'd feel terrible, and so would you."

He looked down in defeat and then said, "Okay. See you."

"Bye." I watched him stumble up the front steps before pulling away from the curb. I wasn't sure if Finn's attempt to go home with me, as well as the car lean-in, could constitute a real ego-boosting for myself. Of course, he was gorgeous. But he was also an alcoholic, among other things. Being under the influence, he may have thought I had three eyes and a horn growing out of my head. *Jesus, huh?* I shook my head. *What a night.*

It was almost two years later before I ran into Finn again. It was a Saturday evening, and Maggie invited me to come up to the city with her. Ryan was now living in another well-known Irish enclave, also known as the Sunset District. They were heading into the Richmond to have some drinks at an Irish sports bar. I could just crash on Ryan's couch and drive home with Maggie in the morning. I was in. A girl's gotta leave the Peninsula sometime, even if it is just to replace one Irish bar with another. Maggie closed up the boutique that night, and we headed to her car. Her cell phone rang, and she answered it.

"Yeah, babe, okay. I just locked up. Yeah, okay. We'll see you in a bit."

She clicked off her phone, looked at me, and said, "Finn's coming tonight."

I admit my stomach jumped. I wasn't sure why. I mean, sure, I'd replayed the car lean-in scenario a "few" times in my mind, wondering what might've happened had I decided to go against all ethics and defy logic by making out with him. Of course, I'd then always come to my senses and heave a collective sigh of relief. I'd done the right thing. Finn was a sweet guy, but he was clearly troubled and absolutely, if not unintentionally, trouble.

And I had my own troubles, one being that I kept getting older. Yes, a law of nature, I realized, but I wasn't ready to embrace it. See, it would've been easy if everyone I hung out with was actually my age. Then I'd at least have people to commiserate with over impending gray hair and wrinkles. *But no.* All my friends my age had gone and gotten married and/or had kids. They pretty much limited themselves to couples' dinners and our monthly book club night. I'm not condemning them. Perhaps, if I were married, I too would turn into a hermit type who loathed being out later than eleven o'clock on a Saturday night and who only preferred the company of other grown-ups (i.e., married people). If you're married, don't hate me. Secretly, you know it's true.

I loved my married friends, but I just didn't belong to the married club. And that was okay with me. I was on my own track—to where, I wasn't sure, but to somewhere. However, in the meantime, what was an unattached sociable girl to do? I'll tell you, simply hang out with other friends who were seven to ten years younger. Maggie happened to be seven years younger, but we got on fabulously. Of course, she erred on the more mature side, while I erred on the more immature side, so I guess this worked to our friendship's advantage. While we became good friends, we spent quite a bit of time hanging out. And of course, since Maggie was dating Ryan, he was naturally included in the mix. But I never felt like I was a third wheel. If anything, I'm sure, at times Ryan felt like he was the third wheel.

And now here was Ryan inviting Finn, crashing our evening out.

Well, I couldn't blame Ryan for having friends, now, could I? I was torn between excitement that Finn was tagging along and dread.

"Jesus is coming tonight?" I asked with an arched brow.

Maggie snickered, "Yes, but don't worry about Jesus. I told him you've had enough drama. Anyway, he's been kinda chatting some girl up lately. It's cute. I wouldn't worry about him."

Thank God. However, I found myself a tad disappointed. Well, wasn't Finn the fickle one? He could just forget about me so soon? Never mind that the almost-make-out situation had happened two years prior, and I was pretty sure he had only been spurred on by a plentitude of alcoholic beverages, but still. Oh, I was too old for him anyway. No, wait, he was too young for me!

"We'll just swing by Finn's and pick him up and be on our way," said Maggie.

Pick him up? Did that mean he was spending the night too? Most likely, since it was a pricey cab ride back from the city. Well, I didn't care how cute Jesus was; I still had dibs on Ryan's couch. He was going to have to fend for himself and stay away from me. Oddly, I was still nervous and in a slightly giddy way.

When Finn got in the backseat, I turned back to say hello. He nodded shyly and said in his soft voice, "Hello, Giuliana." It was notably awkward. I wondered if he was thinking about the last time the two of us had been in a car together—that is, if he even remembered. There was a very good chance that he didn't and that the awkwardness was all in my head. But I let Finn and Maggie do all the talking on the drive up anyway. Hopefully the weirdness would eventually subside after a couple of drinks.

Ryan was waiting for us with a round of drinks.

"Hi, love." He kissed Maggie. He then looked at Finn and me, saying, "We're having a bit of a celebration tonight, you two."

He paused, and Maggie held up her left hand, saying, "We got engaged!"

"What? When? Congratulations!" I said, grabbing Maggie.

"Jesus, it's about time," Finn said. "Congratulations." He shook Ryan's hand.

"Anyway, we're glad you two are here, because I want to ask you to be one of my bridesmaids." Maggie smiled warmly.

"Of course," I said without hesitation.

"And I'd like you to be my best man," Ryan said to Finn.

"I'd be honored," said Finn.

"Well, that was easy." Maggie laughed.

"I'll drink to that!" Ryan raised his glass, and we joined him.

Finn said, "I've the next round."

The celebrating was on. We had a few, and I was sure we'd be having a few more. I didn't know what to make of Finn and his drinking. He didn't seem like an out-of-control drunk. And according to most, his drinking, as of late, was "under control" (i.e., he hadn't gone so overboard that he'd slipped back into drug use). If people wanted to categorize that as a success, well, that was their prerogative, I guessed. It seemed like a messed-up way of thinking, but it wasn't my business. I barely knew Finn. And what could I say? He didn't appear to be drinking any more than the rest of us. Of course, we were all drinking a lot. Did that mean we all had drinking problems too? I didn't linger too long on that somewhat hypothetical question. I mean, I had to finish my drink, since Maggie was about to get the next round.

Before she left the table, she asked Finn, "So what's going on with that girl you've been talking to?"

"Oh, yeah, tell us about the girlfriend," I said, and I meant that in a strictly friendly way. The drinks had been flowing and the conversation too, so I figured it'd be okay to ask. There had been no romantic overtones between Finn and me, so I figured, why not?

"I don't have a girlfriend," Finn said almost angrily, looking at me in annoyance.

Maggie shrugged and went off to the bar.

"Um, okay." What was his problem now? Great, now was it going to be weird because I'd asked a simple question? I headed off to the bathroom. When in doubt, always flee to the bathroom. The long line for the ladies' room will hopefully give the situation time to diffuse itself.

The bar was crowded, and it was a good ten minutes before I made my way back toward our table. As I got closer, I saw Finn standing in the middle of the bar, just staring toward the direction of the bathroom, from whence I was coming. He stood there with a look of determination upon his face, scanning the crowd while people milled about him and around him, making their way to the bar, as if he was waiting for someone. If I didn't know any better, I'd have said he was looking for me and at me. As I moved forward, it became apparent he was, indeed, looking at me. But he couldn't be. But he was. I looked over my shoulder nervously to see if there was perchance someone else he was looking at. For all the crowdedness in the bar, there was no one behind me.

My stomach jumped. What was he doing? Why was he standing there, staring at me like that? And what was I going to do? There was no way to get to our table without going right toward and past Finn. When I came close, I gave a weak smile. *Jeez!* Had I known he was so sensitive, I never would've made the girlfriend comment. I aimed to pass by, but as I did, Finn threw one arm around me, grabbed my face with the other, and planted a long kiss on my lips. Well, the kiss lasted probably about four seconds tops. In those four seconds, though, time felt as if it had stopped.

And of course, in those four mere seconds, I obsessed, since that's what I do. What was Finn doing? I'd just pissed him off, I'd thought. An alcoholic who was ten years younger was kissing me! And I sort of liked it. *Oh my God!* Maybe someone had dared Finn to kiss an "old lady" in the bar, and he'd chosen me! Oh, this was awful. *But not that bad.* Finn was cute. Really cute. Wait, I was kissing someone in a bar—the ultimate of tackiness. I didn't do that sort of thing!

I pushed myself away from Finn and looked up at him with what I'm sure was obvious shock. He looked down at me and said matter-of-factly, "Well, I finally got that kiss I've been waiting for."

Then he grinned shyly at me. *Huh?* He'd been waiting two years to kiss me? There had to be some mistake, some type of explanation. I'd never had the greatest self-esteem when it came to men, and mine had taken a serious nosedive while dating Seamus and had yet to fully recover. Therefore, this was weird to me. I figured I wasn't exactly the type whom boys pined over. Finn wistfully (yeah, right) waiting two years to kiss me was some kind of joke. And the joke had to be on me.

We headed back to the table where Ryan was, while sneaking sideways glances at each other. *What is happening?* I sat pensively at the table while the boys talked among themselves. When Maggie approached with our drinks, I practically pounced on her. I hissed under my breath, "You will not believe what just happened!"

"Oh God, what? What did Ryan do?" Maggie asked with a look of alarm.

"Not Ryan!" I described the slow-motion, crowds-parting, movie-like kiss that had just occurred.

"Wow," Maggie said, shaking her head. "I turn my back to get drinks, and look what I miss!"

"Seriously, I don't understand," I said in disbelief.

Maggie shrugged and smiled mischievously. "Well, we'll just see what happens tonight. Of course, I have a feeling I already know."

"What?" I asked dumbly and then looked over at Finn. He was staring at me. Our eyes locked for a moment, and I looked away fast. I felt my face grow hot. Maggie laughed. It was all over.

On the car ride back to Ryan's, when Finn put his arm around me and kissed me, I didn't resist. When Ryan and Maggie stumbled off to Ryan's room to go to sleep, the two of us were left to stare at each other—me on the couch, Finn in the easy chair. I already knew, though, that I didn't stand a chance of hogging the couch that night. Finn would be right there beside me.

In the morning I left with Maggie, who had to be back to open the store on time. I didn't feel it necessary to wake Finn, snoring on the couch, to say good-bye. I knew I'd see him again sometime. And really the whole previous evening had been so random. We couldn't repeat it if we tried. Yes, I felt the likelihood of anything more transpiring between Finn and me was pretty slim.

As soon as we got in the car, Maggie turned to me and said expectantly, "Well? What happened? I'm dying to know."

I smiled and shrugged. "He's ... really cute."

"Yeah, yeah, I know. So what happened?"

"Nothing, we just made out and then passed out," I said.

Maggie said, "So I have to know. Is Finn a good kisser?"

"Yes," I said. He was.

Maggie exhaled. "Oh, thank God. I was going to be so disappointed if he was terrible. He's so hot. It just would've been a total letdown."

I agreed. My mind drifted.

"You're gorgeous," he'd murmured into my ear while we squeezed ourselves together to keep from falling off the couch.

"Aw, come on. It's dark in here. You can't even see me," I joked.

He sat up and said, "Giuliana, I know what you look like. You're gorgeous."

His compliment thrilled me, because I thought he was gorgeous too. But compliments always made me feel nervous and self-conscious. Acknowledging them, to me, had always seemed like open vanity and arrogance. I'm not sure why, since I am actually vain. And, just like the next person, who doesn't want to hear something wonderful said about themselves? Yet I'd learned to deflect very well.

"You're not so bad yourself," I answered.

It was dark, but I could see him looking at me. He grabbed hold of my hand. "Your hands are so soft."

Again with the compliments. I was flustered, and no quick one-liners came to mind. And his hands weren't soft, so I left it at that.

Maggie was speaking to me, but I hadn't heard a word she'd said.

"I'm sorry, what?" I asked blankly.

"Did Finn ask for your number?" she said again.

"Oh, no, no," I said quickly.

Maggie sighed. "He's just so shy. I'll talk to Ryan later and get the scoop."

I was sure there wouldn't be anything much to report, but I still waited with anticipation for her call that afternoon.

"I just got off the phone with Ryan," Maggie said later on. "Apparently, Finn has had a crush on you for quite some time."

"What?" I said in disbelief. This was an interesting new development.

"Yes," Maggie continued. "He asked Ryan to ask what you thought of him and said he thought you were a sound girl."

In Irish speak, being "sound" is a good thing.

"Huh." I wasn't sure what to say.

"Are you sure Ryan didn't dare him to kiss me in the bar?" I asked, ever the realist.

"What?" Maggie asked.

I explained, "Maybe he dared Finn to kiss an older woman or something."

"Please." I could practically see Maggie rolling her eyes over the phone. "He likes you. I like you two together. This could be really good."

Finn and me? A pair of mismatched misfits was what we were.

I laughed ruefully. "Right, two messed-up people."

"Yeah, but maybe you could help each other," Maggie said thoughtfully. If therapy hadn't been successful in fixing me (of course, I'd been the one to end it and much too early), I doubted anyone else would be able to help me cope with all my looming neuroses. And I didn't know that I wanted to take on someone like Finn, who needed more help than I could ever give. I was a nurturing person by nature but felt that part of myself had been bled dry during the Seamus years. What I needed was someone who was steady and reliable, as opposed to being a walking time bomb. I was certain that Finn was of the time bomb variety.

So the romance began anyway. My mother has frequently told me I'm that person who just doesn't believe the wet paint sign until I've actually put my hand in the wet paint and smeared it all over myself, thus proving that, yes, indeed, the paint was wet. And, yes, it's usually in reference to my romances gone awry. She's right, I'll say.

The romance commenced, and much to everyone's disappointment (including yours, I'll assume), I did not become some sort of magical beacon of light in Finn's dark, hazy world of drinking and drugs. To this day, I have no idea what I was to him, but I was not his savior. In fact, sadly, I was more than likely one of his many enablers for some time. I drank with him. We all did. We certainly didn't encourage him to drink, but we didn't discourage him either. It was assumed that he'd heard it all before, so what was the point in lecturing? Finn appeared to be keeping his drinking in reasonable check, as well—"reasonable check" being he hadn't been taken in by the cops for passing out on bus stop benches, he was still showing up to work with Ryan every day, and as far as we knew, he was not using drugs (his favorite being of the white powdery kind). Maybe, we thought naively, he could drink and be able to handle it.

A few months passed. Finn made a habit of showing up when I was out with Maggie and Ryan, and that was it. We stuck together the whole night. He came to my school auction with me and helped move me into the apartment in the Sunset District I was going to share with Maggie. I guessed he liked me, or so Ryan and Maggie told me. And I liked him. Aside from being all-around lovely, he was very sweet and had a gentleness about him. At the same time, he was ten years younger, and I couldn't help wondering where this was going. I mean, I didn't have all the time in the world, did I? Oh, yeah, and there was that pesky drinking problem, not to mention the drug addiction that I'd yet to witness firsthand but that I knew was quietly bubbling under the surface.

On the night Finn moved me into the apartment, I decided to address the question of us, because frankly I was confused. So, yes, I became one of those girls who asks that question. A big no-no in my book, but I figured this was not a normal situation and, therefore, the normal rules of question asking did not apply.

"What is going on with us?" I asked plainly and not in a whiny way at all.

Finn looked at me seriously and said, "I like you a lot."

"I like you too," I answered.

"Giuliana …" He hesitated a moment before saying, "I think the two of us could either be really great together or really bad together."

I had to admit I agreed with him. There could be no in-betweens. I had major depression issues, and although I hadn't had a black episode in a while, the amount of drinking I was doing didn't help. Finn, as we all knew, was always a step away from crashing and burning. Yet I felt I knew him and could relate to him in so many ways. We were very different but very alike. It was strange. Could two misfits help each other?

Before I could respond, Finn said in an upbeat voice, "You know what? Let's give it a go. What do you think?"

I thought it sounded like a tall order, but I said okay because as pessimistic as I am, I believed there was something there.

"You're gorgeous," he said for the hundredth time.

"So are you."

When a week went by after our "Let's be a couple" chat, and I still hadn't heard from Finn, I automatically assumed he'd been scared off. I became distressed and depressed, yet not necessarily surprised.

What did I expect? I was old—well, comparatively speaking. Finn could gallivant around with any young tramp-stamped thing in the bars if he wanted to. Why would he want me? And what had I been thinking when I asked about the status of our relationship? As if there was one. Why had I gone against my better (and older and wiser) judgment? I obsessed on and on. Yes, leave it to me to make this all about myself.

Caving in with acute curiosity, I told Maggie I hadn't heard from Finn all week. She immediately called Ryan, since he saw him every day at work. She got off the phone and said, "Well, not good news. Apparently, Lydia called Finn on Monday, and they got in some kind of argument. He was pretty upset, and he hasn't shown up to work since."

Oh, no.

"He's not answering his phone, and the truck's not at the house. No one knows where he is." Maggie closed her eyes and sighed. She then said, "Here we go again. I pray he's not using, but when he goes missing, that's not a good sign."

Damn that Lydia. Could she have picked any worse timing to rile up Finn? Actually, I'm really not that self-centered. My first thought was that I was completely horrified at the notion of him being somewhere doing drugs and whatever else with no one knowing where he was. God only knew what could happen. Yes, I'd be lying if I said I wasn't totally disappointed that he was gone, and we obviously would not be giving the relationship a go. But there was consolation in the fact that it had been so short-lived. There had been no tumultuous disaster. What little still remained of my post-Seamus heart hadn't been ripped to shreds, just tugged at a bit. But I was still intact. And in some small way, it was comforting to know that it really wasn't me who had driven Finn away. And as much as everyone would've liked to have blamed her, it wasn't Lydia either. Her pushing Finn's buttons was just another excuse for him to flee. And then I came back to. *Damn that Lydia anyway. Oh, the timing.*

A year and a half later, Ryan and Maggie got married back in County Mayo. I was one of the bridesmaids, remember? Finn was not in the wedding. After a few more horrendous downward spirals, he went through another rehab program and decided it would be best to keep himself out of temptation's way and stay home. I'd heard he was living in a safe house and was doing well. Other than that, I'd seen or heard nothing from him since the night he'd moved me into the apartment.

Some months later, Finn called and left me a message. He was just calling to say hi. He hoped I was well and asked if I would call him when I got the chance. I was, of course, surprised and slightly baffled. Did I want to talk to him? I thought so.

"Maggie, Finn called and left a message asking how I was and to call him." I had stopped in the store to share the news personally.

"Oh, he did. He was talking to Ryan yesterday and asked if you thought he was an asshole and could he call you? I didn't want to tell you in case he didn't call. You know him."

I did, I thought.

"Did you call him back?" she asked.

"No, but I will."

"Giuliana, how are ya?" he said when I called that night. *Oh, that voice.* It'd been a long time since I'd heard it.

"Good! How are you? How are you doing?"

"Great, great. Working a lot and playing a lot of golf, hurling, and football. Keeps me busy, ya know?"

We chatted some more, and then he asked, "So are you busy on Wednesday night? I was wondering … would you like to go to The Iron Door with me for dinner? Everyone is always talking about the filet mignon there, and I'm sick of hearing them. Are you busy?"

I was thankful Finn couldn't see my jaw hit the ground. We'd never been on a date. In fact, we'd never really seen each other outside of some type of drinking environment, whether it was at the bars or someone's birthday party or Ryan's apartment. However, I recovered nicely and accepted the invitation.

"I'll come and pick you up, say, around six thirty. We have a curfew at the house, and I have to be in by nine thirty. Hope that's all right."

It was fine.

"Have a good night, Giuliana."

Wow. I have a date with Finn. And he is picking me up.

I was no longer living in the Sunset District. Maggie and Ryan had graciously told me they didn't mind if I stayed on in the apartment and paid rent, since we were all such good friends. Even though they'd been together eight years and weren't typical newlyweds beginning to play house, I felt they needed their own space. I decided it was best to move out and back to the Peninsula.

I was now living in a large house in swanky Santa Marita with a couple of roommates. One was a finicky older lady who complained a lot and frequently got bent out of shape when my social life didn't involve her. The other roomie was sweet but quite nosey, and whenever I left the house, I had to make sure my bedroom door was closed, or she'd get into all my things. The roomies I speak of were my eighty-seven-year-old grandmother and her beagle, Sadie.

I loved my roomies, of course. It'd been a no-brainer when my grandmother, hearing I was moving out from the city apartment, asked if I'd be willing to move in with her.

"Why don't you move in here? You can have your mother's room," Grandma said one day when I was visiting her.

Before I could answer, she added, "It'd be nice having someone around, having you here."

I countered with "Well, I'd love moving in, but just so you know, I'm not home a lot."

I really wasn't. Between work, the gym, and going out with friends, the amount of time I spent at home (wherever that might be) was small. Best to dispel any notions my grandmother might've had about me spending every weekend evening at home watching *Wheel of Fortune* and *Touched by an Angel* reruns with her.

Grandma patted my hand. "That's all right. It'll just be nice knowing you're here. You can earn your keep by taking me to the store every once in a while and bringing the paper in in the morning. These knees of mine are killing me!"

So it was settled. I agreed to the unwritten contract. It was like coming home anyway. My sister and I had spent our entire childhood at my grandparents' home, more than we ever did at our actual home fifteen minutes away. I needed a place to go for the time being, and Grandma needed me. Although she had all her faculties (minus her hearing and bad knees), I worried about her being on her own. And I would have tons of space too. This would be a good move for both of us.

Never mind that I was approaching the end of my midthirties and would be living with my grandmother. Yes, I said *never mind*.

So, Finn was going to be picking me up. This would be interesting. It would be interesting for oh so many reasons. The first one was that I hadn't seen Finn in about two years. And he would be completely sober. Mind you, I had actually seen him for short periods of time when he wasn't inebriated. But this was definitely taking it to another level. It was exciting and good, but it was scary too. Would he like me as his sober self? Would I like him as his sober self? Had it all only been a drunken thing?

The next thing of "interest" was my age and the fact that I was now living with Grandma. I likened myself to a pinball, shooting back and forth from one family member to the next. I'd lived at home when I was dating Seamus and had ended up staying there for quite some time when my mom became sick. With my sister married and out of the house, I hadn't felt I could leave my mom. You know that darn Responsible First Child Syndrome.

I'd finally felt it was time to spread my wings and lead some sort of a grown-up life and had moved to the city. That had been great, but as luck would have it, my roommate got married. Apparently, life moved on for others. People got married, bought homes, had kids—that is, other people did. I, on the other hand, seemed to be in a constant state of Nowheresville (now my grandmother's abode). Yet, however odd others might have viewed my new living situation, deep down, for whatever reason, I had a feeling that maybe this was where I was supposed to be. And really, Finn was now living in a safe house for alcoholics that had a curfew. He certainly wouldn't be judging the fact that he was picking me up from Grandma's. At least I didn't have a curfew, although I'm sure Grandma would've preferred that I'd kept to one.

And last, but not least of interest, was that not only was I living with Grandma, but Mom temporarily was too. My mother had taken a spill at home and fractured her fibula. As a result, she was pretty much couch-ridden and needed a lot of help doing even the simplest of household things. Sad to say, but Grandma, even with her bad knees, was in better shape and could somewhat help out, watching over Mom. I mean, you'd think a mother would gladly take care of her wounded child, even if the child was in her sixties. Once a mother, always a mother, right?

Grandma readily took Mom in but, once there, made it a living hell, acting very put out. My mom, in turn, didn't want to be there either. Let's just say the two of them had always gotten on each other's nerves. It was all compounded by the fact that neither of them could drive, and they were trapped with each other all day, until I could get home. It was like living with the Odd Couple, and I was the unfortunate mediator. Most of the time, I retreated to the back of the house. If I could have, I would have moved back into my mom's house for the peace and quiet, but leaving the two of them alone would have been a bit hazardous and someone's life would have been at risk for sure.

So, Finn's pickup was going to be … well, interesting. Hopefully, Grandma's hearing aids would be on the fritz, and she wouldn't hear the doorbell. I didn't have to worry about Mom, since she'd already met Finn years before and wouldn't be hobbling fast enough on her crutches to make it out to the front room for a peek at him this time. I was all dressed up—pencil skirt, black jacket, and high Pedro Garcia heels. I mean, this was a date to a good restaurant. The Iron Door (thank God for me, the restaurant snob) was no Macaroni Grill or El Torito. And of course, this was Finn. Enough said.

I wondered what Finn would be wearing. His wardrobe was strictly limited to a pair of Tommy Hilfiger carpenter jeans and a rotation of a few different rugby shirts or sweatshirts, with running shoes or his work boots. I was pretty sure I'd seen every piece of clothing he had.

The doorbell rang. I inadvertently jumped. Why was I so nervous? The dog was going ballistic, barking at my side as I opened the door. Finn stood on the step underneath the porch light. He looked a bit older, in a weathered, worn way. And was that some gray in his closely shorn hair? He looked the same but different. And he was dressed up too. He wore a leather jacket (which he no doubt had borrowed) over a button-up shirt with khakis and dress shoes. I was a bit stunned and speechless. He was dressed up. No doubt about it though, he was still beautiful.

"Hi." He smiled a shy half smile.

"Hi," I said, probably trying not to smile too hard. We hugged.

"Do you need the front door key?" And there was Grandma,

standing right behind me. Apparently, her aids were working just fine tonight. Finn and I quickly disconnected ourselves.

"I'll just bring my garage door opener," I said hastily.

Ignoring my answer, Grandma peeked over my shoulder and said, "Well, hello."

"Grandma, this is Finn. Finn, this is my grandmother." I made the necessary introductions.

"Hello. Nice to meet you." Finn nodded calmly, as if he picked up his dates from their grandmother's houses all the time.

"I'll go get the garage door opener. Be right back," I said.

I scurried off as best I could in four-and-a-half-inch heels. As I did, I heard Grandma say almost coyly, "Finn, you'll have to come in and see our Christmas tree!"

I rolled my eyes. The old Christmas tree ploy—as if he'd never seen a Christmas tree before. Before I could get into the kitchen, out came my mom on her crutches. I'd never seen her move so fast, with or without her crutches. *Jesus, and all because I have a date.* It wasn't like I never had dates. But it was Finn. I knew he was worth a peek, but ...

"Seriously?" I muttered to my mother as I scooted past her.

"What? Why can't I come out and see him?" my mom asked in an irritable whisper. Clearly, I really needed to get my own place.

I came back out and waited as my mom chatted with Finn. Sadie sniffed his pants, like the good beagle she was. Grandma interrupted loudly, as was customary, since she couldn't always hear people's conversations. "Where are you two going for dinner?"

Finn looked over politely and said, "The Iron Door. Ever been there?"

"Oh, yes, many times. That's a nice restaurant."

"That's what I hear. Well, should we be off?" Finn looked at me seriously.

"Sure," I said, and I hoped I didn't sound too relieved. I mean, any longer and my grandma would've grabbed her camera and turned this into some awkward Christmas Formal photo shoot.

"See you later on," I called. "We'll go out the front, and I have the garage door opener for when I get back." I waited at the door for Finn.

He said to the ladies, "It was very nice to meet you and very nice to see you again, Mrs. Lombardi. Oh, and you've a lovely Christmas tree."

Grandma beamed. "Well, thank you. Come back again now! Have a good time!"

I closed the door behind us. We looked at each other briefly, and then Finn said, "Your grandmother is so cute. And your mother's looking well, even on the crutches and all."

How sweet. I held off on making any disparaging remarks about my roommates, Ernie and Bert.

Onto the date! Onto The Iron Door! We checked in with the maître d' and were escorted gallantly to our table. If I'd ever felt I was old, I was in good company that night. Actually, I felt pleasantly young and spry, seeing as how the majority of the clientele were well into their eighties.

We sat down, and I joked, "You might be the youngest one here tonight."

Finn chuckled and answered, "I'd say we both are. There must be an early-bird special."

The waiter approached rapidly. No doubt, he had been well trained to serve the blue hairs promptly. Obviously, we weren't his typical customers, but Finn did have a curfew.

"Good evening, can I get you two anything to drink? Here's the wine list."

Oh God. Drinks? I hadn't thought about that at all. I surely would have loved a glass of wine or two (I was still quite nervous and shy), but I couldn't drink in front of Finn, could I?

"I'll have a Coke," Finn said.

The waiter and Finn looked at me expectantly.

"Just water, thanks," I said quickly.

The waiter left, and Finn said, "Giuliana, have whatever you want to drink. Just order what you'd normally order."

Wine really sounded good. But I couldn't …

"That's not going to bother you?" I asked skeptically.

"I've been sober for nine months now. It won't bother me a bit," he answered assuredly.

I wanted to believe that, but I had a hard time doing so. An alcoholic forced to watch others drink in front of him? That'd be like throwing me into the middle of Barneys shoe department and having me sit on my hands and feet while my friends tried on and bought shoes. I decided to pass on the glass of wine.

"No, no, I'm fine, really," I said.

"Giuliana please, have whatever you'd like," he insisted.

To appease him, I said, "Well, if the waiter comes back again, maybe ..."

As luck would have it, the waiter didn't come back to us for quite some time. He was too busy shuffling back and forth to the Golden Girls at the next table. By then, we were hungry and ordered an appetizer.

"Will we try the escargot, Giuliana? Have you ever had them?"

"No," I admitted.

"Let's try them," Finn said in almost-childlike excitement.

We tried them.

"Not bad, salty, but a bit like chicken, eh?" Finn stated.

We talked. We talked about him working for his uncle's plaster-and-stucco company. We talked about golf. He asked me about school and my class. We talked about his son. He told me he was down to one pack of cigarettes a day. We ate. He was satisfied with the filet mignon he'd heard so much about. We talked some more. We were still a little bit shy, both of us. I was okay with it being slightly awkward, because that's what it's supposed to be like when you're on a first date with someone you actually like.

He drove me home, parked in the driveway, and walked me as far as the open garage door.

Before I could thank him for dinner, Finn asked, "So, do you want to go to the driving range on Friday night?"

A second date already? He wasn't wasting any time. I wasn't complaining, though.

"Yeah, sure, that sounds fun. Thanks for dinner," I said.

"You're very welcome. Thanks for going with me. I'll talk to you before Friday." He leaned in, kissed me on the lips, and then walked back to his truck. I waved and went inside. By the time I'd gotten back to my room, there was a text from Finn

"Sweet dreams Giuliana."

If I was able to sleep at all.

The next day, I called Maggie, as she was waiting for the blow-by-blow account of the date.

"What was he wearing?" she asked cautiously.

I described Finn's evening attire.

Maggie said, "Oh, yeah, the khakis, I've seen those. Okay, good. Leather jacket? He for sure borrowed that from his dad." Yes, we were all quite familiar with Finn's sparse wardrobe ensembles.

"And how was it?" Maggie continued.

"It was fun. He was so … cute," I gushed.

"You keep saying he's *cute*. You make him sound like a five-year-old," Maggie said.

"Well, he is a lot younger," I quipped.

"*Please,*" said Maggie in annoyance.

"All right, let me rephrase. He's still totally gorgeous."

"Thank you. That's much better," Maggie said, relief in her voice.

"We're going to the driving range on Friday night," I added.

"Wow, nice work, Finn. And good job, Giuliana," Maggie said.

She replied, "You know, if you two had kids, they'd be beautiful."

"Let's not get ahead of ourselves," I said quickly.

"Right."

Again, Finn picked me up and shot the breeze with my roomies for a few minutes before we took off to the local driving range. We hit a few buckets of balls in companionable silence, commenting every now and then on our swings, hits, and (my) slices. On our way back to the car, Finn pulled up his sleeve and said, "What do ya think of my new tattoo?"

Covering the whole inside of his lower arm was a picture of a woman, and "In Loving Memory, Gran," was inscribed around it in dark ink. I'm not a tattoo person. They're so permanent. But I'm not opposed to other people having them, as long as they have meaning and aren't a spur-of-the-drunken-moment "Awesome idea, I'm in Mazatlán on Spring Break!" stupid type of tattoo.

Finn's tattoo was not stupid. It was a tribute to his grandmother who'd died a few years back.

"It looks amazing," I said honestly.

"Thanks," he said proudly.

On the drive home, he said, "Do you want to go bowling on Saturday?"

As much fun as the driving range was, I'm ten times better at bowling. *A chance to redeem myself and my lack of sportiness with a golf club?* I was up for it. I was having fun with Finn, and there was no alcohol involved. It was an empowering feeling.

It was a typical workweek, meaning it was slow. To say I was looking forward to the weekend would've been an understatement. Of course, I had reason to feel a heightened sense of anticipation. Let's be frank—you're never too old to get excited about the weekend or about seeing someone you like. If you are not excited, either you have the most wonderful and fulfilling job in the universe or you are dead. I was not dead. I was very much alive and, therefore, very excited.

And just to keep my spirits at their most enthusiastic, every night, Finn would send me a text asking how I was, wishing me a good night, and the like. If I didn't know better, I'd say he liked me and was looking forward to seeing me too. Funny, with all the guys I'd dated or been involved with in the past, who were "stable, responsible, well educated, and put together," none of them had ever taken the time to touch base with me every day. So, this smallest of efforts did not go unappreciated, and I took it as a good sign.

Finally, *finally*, Saturday rolled around. Before I could even begin to think about the impending bowling date, I received a text from Finn saying, "I've got a cold. Will have to call off bowling. Sorry will call ya later."

I was disappointed for sure. What was to be the apex of my week had instantly become obsolete.

A couple of days went by, and I heard nothing from Finn. Then a week went by and then another, and still no word. Christmas was approaching fast, and I doubted if ever I'd hear from him, yet I couldn't take it personally. But I worried and wondered if he was all right. The holidays were always rough, even for those without powerful addictions. Would he make it through them? Or had Finn caved again to his demons?

I was on Christmas vacation, and while I hadn't completely stopped thinking about Finn, I had definitely laid to rest the idea of his getting in touch with me or with my reaching out to him. It was best to let it go. One night I tossed and turned, unable to sleep. I checked my phone for the time. It was well after midnight. And there was a text from Finn.

"I am so sorry. You are so great but I don't know how to be sober around you. I'm going to start drinking again."

I could've taken that personally. Was I so scary that he had to drink to be around me? Did I only seem fun and attractive when others were under the influence? But the mature side of me knew better and luckily took over. It wasn't me that scared Finn. It was living that frightened him.

I quickly wrote back. "Don't worry about us. Take care of yourself first. But please don't start drinking."

There was no response from him. I frantically dialed his number. No answer. I cried. I couldn't help it. But I didn't cry for myself. I cried for him. And I knew I wouldn't hear from him again. No one would and for quite some time, I was sure. There was nothing I could do. There was nothing anyone could do. I turned out the light and went to sleep.

"The Funny Thing Is ... I Met Someone in Venice."

Sorry to say, I didn't meet someone in Venice. Right, how disappointing. But anyway, I'll get to that later. About Rich Calamari ...

Rich Calamari was a year ahead of me in college. Not only was he in Dante Prosecco's class, but he was one of his Kappa Sigma fraternity brothers. I had quite a few friends who were Kappa Sigs even before I'd met and started dating Dante, but I'd never seen or met Rich. I knew nothing about him. My first introduction, if you will, to Rich was when I called Dante's apartment one night. Someone answered the phone (no voice I recognized) and said tartly, "House of Dildos, how can I help you?"

I obviously thought I'd dialed the wrong number. *House of Dildos? Is there one around campus? Eek.* Don't ask me how I knew what a dildo was either. I can only surmise that going to an all-girl Catholic high school led us young ladies to hold some rather raunchy discussions at the lunchroom tables now and again. Still, I was slightly mortified.

"Uh, is Dante there?" I asked uncertainly.

"Yeah, hang on a second," the sharp voice said.

Phew, I thought. And then I was mortified once again when I heard the voice on the other end shout, "Yeah, Dante, it's for you. I don't know. I think it's your mom."

I'm not sure if I was more concerned with having sounded like a mom or that whoever had answered the phone had spoken so brazenly the word "dildos" to a potential mom.

Dante got on the phone. "Hey!"

"Who was that?" I asked warily.

"Oh, that was Rich Calamari. You know Rich?" he asked.

"No," I said gladly.

"Oh, he's been studying abroad in Italy for the last quarter. He just got back. You'll meet him at some of our Kappa Sig events."

I wasn't sure I wanted to meet him. He had already somewhat insulted me by assuming I was Dante's mom, not that she wasn't a lovely person and all. I thought I could do without being introduced to this Calamari character.

But as Dante had prophesied, it eventually happened at a Kappa Sig party of some sort. And, truth be told, he scared me. Rich was scary—well, not in a horror-movie type of way. He was an upperclassman (granted, only a measly year older, but need I say more?). He wasn't one of those intimidatingly gorgeous, yet rakish, upperclassmen who hung out in the Kappa Sig kitchen manning the kegs while blatantly checking you out (even if you had a boyfriend). No, Rich wasn't really cute. He was on the shorter side, with shoulder-length dark-red wavy hair, which he sometimes wore in a ponytail. That alone, right there, was cause enough for me not to be attracted to him at all. He wore glasses and, being a redhead, had that freckled type of skin. I heard he played keyboard and drums in a band. There was definitely a rockerish vibe to his look, as opposed to the typical preppy Kappa Sigma style. I wasn't into it. I mean, there was Dante. But even so, in my youthful shallowness and intimidation, I wouldn't have looked twice.

To add to his interesting attributes, Rich was intelligent and witty and had quite a crude and bitingly sarcastic sense of humor. Being the painfully shy sophomore I was, I didn't know what to make of him. Was he going to be nice, or would he spew some sort of mockery at my expense? He was quite capable of it. I kept my conversations with him to a minimum—best not to give him any sort of material to use against me. Not like he had a personal vendetta toward me—on the contrary. In fact, I was probably no more than an inconsequential blip on Rich's radar.

All in all, I didn't have much to do with him while dating Dante. It was when I began dating Patrick (another Kappa Sigma) my senior year that I got to know Rich better and wasn't totally freaked out by him. Rich had graduated the year before, but being a native to the Bay Area, he still lived and worked in the area. As a result, he occasionally hung out with the Kappa Sigs who were in my class and friends of his; therefore, I too would end up hanging out with him. I began to appreciate his dry sense of humor. He was quirky but really funny. But I still didn't think he was cute. Let's not forget at that time I had my (gay) boyfriend.

Unfortunately, I had to graduate within the preferable four-year time frame and leave college behind. Oh, how I would've loved to have been one of those people who'd jauntily switched majors halfway through and ended up having to stay longer, thus avoiding the real world. But no. And by the way, the real world sucked. In the real world, your best buddies didn't live next door or upstairs, people didn't throw spontaneous keggers or progressive drinking parties on a Wednesday night, and you had to (blech) earn a living. But first you had to actually find a job. Don't get me started on that.

Yeah, the real world was a totally depressing letdown after four years of carefree (excluding finals and thesis time) bliss. I've never been one for change, but like it or not, it had to happen. I missed college fiercely and had major withdrawal. Therefore, every so often in my first year out, I gladly went back to my old campus if one of my friends was having a party. But I always left feeling depressed, knowing that I had to return to my mature(ish), noncollegiate life.

Marie called me one day. She was living in the city, and we still hung out. I frequently crashed at her place in Cow Hollow whenever I came up to the city for a night out. Her reason for calling was that Fall Homecoming at our alma mater was approaching. Aside from my first postgraduation year, I hadn't gone back much. We were now four years out. It could've been a million though; time seemed to have passed so quickly.

"Who's going? Will we even know anyone?" I asked cautiously. *Key questions,* I thought.

As usual, Marie had a good answer for both. "It'll be fun. It's the fifth-year homecoming reunion for the class ahead of us, so there'll be tons of people there we know."

True. Her Delta Gamma sorority sisters from that class would be there. Still, I wasn't really close friends with too many of them. I didn't know how long I could hang with all the DG reminiscing.

Marie continued, "Oh, and blah, blah, blah … will be there.

Probably ..." She rattled off a bunch of names, all of whom we'd been friends with.

"It'd be really fun to see everyone!" Marie ended her spiel.

Yeah, it would, I thought.

I had to hand it to Marie. Somehow she always knew my selling points. I was in. Yes, I am ashamed to admit I was actually swayed into going for ... the guys (and *of course* to see my alma mater). Well, the cherished drinking establishment, The Tavern, was somewhat part of campus, wasn't it? That counted, right? That's where everyone was sure to eventually conglomerate anyway.

We went. After having a few beers and chatting with various people in the university gardens, we were off to The Tavern. We parked across the street, and I felt a bit queasy as we approached the front entrance. I'd always had a love–hate relationship with The Tavern. Let me explain. As freshmen and sophomores, you'd rarely venture into The Tavern because a) you needed a fake ID (or a real ID, should you be of age), and b) only upperclassmen hung out there. Enough said. Basically, it felt off-limits unless you were perhaps dating an upperclassman.

Therefore, aside from random frat parties going on, you were more or less confined to hitting O'Neill's, the other bar, which was literally on campus, where of course you also needed said (fake) ID to get in. Don't ask me to explain this one, but somehow everyone in my freshman class had obtained fake IDs. I'm not going to lie. I was one of them. I wouldn't be surprised if the person in charge of this little business was now a very wealthy venture capitalist, because there was serious money to be made off of us party-hungry freshmen. I'm pretty sure most of the whole class had them. That's probably why I don't feel so badly about it (sort of). I mean, none of us were using fake IDs to write fraudulent checks or anything like that. We were just fighting for our lame right to party at O'Neill's.

The IDs weren't stolen, so to speak. I mean, I wasn't flashing a card with a picture of thirty-five-year-old Asian woman, hoping that if the bouncer squinted, he'd possibly think it was me. The fake ID mastermind had found empty ID cards where you could put a real headshot picture of yourself in and then iron it sealed, and presto, you had your ID.

Anyway, after obtaining our "legit" fake IDs we decided that we needn't limit our social setting to O'Neill's. We were going to try out The Tavern. We sauntered over, and I let my friends go ahead of me, as Dave (the long-standing owner) and a young guy stood at the doorway and checked IDs. My friends all got in. When it was my turn, the bouncer took one look at my ID, looked up at me, and said, "This isn't you. Sorry, no."

What? It sounded like a needle scratching a record, and everyone stopped and stared. That's what it felt like. The funny thing was that it was a picture of me. However, being the chickenshit I was, I was not about to argue and draw more attention to myself. I was utterly humiliated.

"Um, okay," I said weakly. Just then, one of my friends peek out the door and said, "What's up?"

I shook my head no and, backing away swiftly, said, "I'm heading back to Duke O'Neill's."

Yeah. That was my first encounter with The Tavern. You could see how I would be scarred from it. From then on, whenever my friends decided to head over to The Tavern, I stayed put wherever I was. There was no way I was setting foot near that place with the crappy luck I had. In fact, when I did actually turn twenty-one and throughout the rest of my college career, whenever I went to The Tavern (which, let's face it, was a lot), I was paranoid that the bouncer would suddenly decide again that it wasn't me on my driver's license and shoo me away. It never happened though, and I was allowed to enter sacred ground. And once I walked over that threshold, I don't think I ever went back to O'Neill's. Hey, I was an upperclassman (finally). This was my turf now. How the tides had turned.

So there's a little Tavern background for you. Anyway, as Marie and I approached the doorway, that old feeling of nausea hit me once again. But I needn't have worried. No one was carding alums back for a reunion, so we pushed ourselves into the crowd. And it was crowded, like any other night I'd ever spent there. The dollar bills and business cards were still pinned to the dirty ceiling, the pool table was still there (though no one was playing), and people were taking shots at the bar. I'm not sure what I'd expected to have happened in the four years I'd been gone (which seemed like an eternity), but I had to admit I was glad it was like stepping back in time. Yes, The Tavern was the same, and all was right in the world.

Before we knew it, we were surrounded by old friends, Rich Calamari being one of them. He still sported the longish hair and his glasses. I still wasn't attracted to him, but I loved talking to him. He was as witty as ever and made me laugh. He was working in computer design at some bigwig Silicon Valley company and was also going to culinary school. Seeing as how I could barely open a laptop without causing it to crash and my cooking hadn't progressed much from boiling Top Ramen, I was impressed.

At the end of the evening, Rich asked for my number. I was a bit caught off guard. I'm not sure why. I mean, we'd been talking all night. What was Rich to think? But the conversation had been nothing of the flirtatious sort—just two friends catching up. What to do? It's always a hairy situation, isn't it? You have a lovely time talking to someone you're not the least bit attracted to, and then when asked for your number, you're completely stunned/horrified. Of course, if you are even slightly attracted to the person, you will undoubtedly act like a complete moron, and, therefore, they won't want your number anyway. But I was of the former and didn't know what to do. I gave him my number (yes, my real number and not a fake one). And by the way, this was before cell phones had come into play, so this was the home phone. He probably wouldn't call anyway, I told myself.

Of course he called. After a few pleasantries, the question arose: "So, Giuliana, are you free this Friday for dinner?" Was I free for dinner? Technically, yes, I was free, because I was in the throes of my first year of teaching, which meant I never made plans since I spent every waking free moment in my classroom doing some type of lesson planning/correcting/bulletin board. I'm a pro now, and this doesn't happen anymore. I mean, you barely see me in the classroom when I'm actually teaching (just kidding, in case my boss is reading this). What I really mean is I've gotten this down pat. By the way, this was also way before Pinterest came along and you could latch onto someone else's creatively crafty teachery lesson plan or art project. Yes, we actually had to come up with our own shit. Because of this, for the first three months of my teaching career none of my friends saw me. It was an actual miracle that Marie had even gotten me to homecoming. But I digress.

So, I was "free," but was I free in the sense that I wanted to be on a dinner date with Rich? I decided I was not. I realize at this point you are probably sniggering to yourself, thinking beggars can't be choosers. I, however, did not see it that way. *Shit,* I thought, *did I lead Rich on? No,* I thought vehemently. I didn't even know how to flirt, much less lead someone on to ask me out. How had this happened, damn it? It was as if it was such a trauma to be asked out to dinner. Oh, shallow youth.

It may sound like I was/am an insensitive person, but actually it's the very opposite. I'm very sensitive and empathetic to any sort of rejection, and I wanted in no way to hurt Rich's feelings. I really did like him, just not like *that.* So, I did what anyone of an ultrasensitive nature might do: I lied.

"Oh, this Friday? Oh, I would love to, but we have report cards that are due on Monday, and it's the first time I've done them, so I have a feeling I'm going to be working on them all weekend," I stammered nervously. Actually, this wasn't a lie. I did have report cards due, and it was going to take me an excruciatingly long time to power through them for the very first time, seeing as how I'd be averaging grades via a handheld calculator (yep, also the days before a computer-run grading system). As to whether I'd need to work around the clock from Friday evening until Sunday night, that was highly unlikely. And I'm sure Rich knew that. He was no dummy. We chitchatted a little longer, and then Rich said, "Well, good luck with your report cards! Talk to you soon." But I knew we wouldn't.

I felt slightly guilty but way more relieved. That had been a close call.

Now let's fast-forward about eight years. I was at a friend's swanky thirty-fifth birthday party at the Fairmont in the city. It was a party to end all parties. For starters, the birthday boy, Tony, was a friend from college, one of my Kappa Sigma buddies. Not only was there an open bar, but Tony's wife had secured the Neil Diamond cover band to perform. Tony was a huge Neil Diamond fan and, therefore, a fanatic of the cover band (as any true Neil Diamond fan would be), and his dream to perform with them for a song or two was apparently going to come true that evening. I arrived with my date, a lovely younger man of the cute, floppy-haired variety whom I'd met a few weeks before at another friend's Christmas party. Bringing a date anywhere (since I never had one) was highly unusual for me, but Floppy-Haired Guy was fun, we'd already been on a few dates, and he lived in the city. It just seemed like the thing to do.

Aside from the coworkers, Tony's family, and random others, it was a veritable college reunion. Not only was Marie with me, but everyone from Delta Gamma/Kappa Sigma whom I'd ever hung out with in college was there. There was even a rumor that Dante Prosecco was supposed to make an appearance.

As a result of the reunion-type atmosphere, a drink was necessary, so Marie, Floppy-Haired Guy, and I headed to the bar. Slouching at the bar with a drink in his hand was Rich Calamari. Hugs were exchanged between Rich and Marie, and Rich and myself, and Floppy-Haired Guy was introduced to Rich, well, as Floppy-Haired Guy.

Rich and I caught up, as if no time had ever passed. I'd been teaching and spending all my summer vacations traveling in Italy. My best friend and I were planning on renting an apartment on the Amalfi Coast when our next summer vacation came around. I was also working on a book based on my travel adventures. I thought I sounded interesting enough and like I had somewhat of a life.

However, I was blown away by what Rich had been up to. He had left the computer company he'd been working for, had finished culinary school, and was now working for a company that opened up high-end designer restaurants and clubs all over the country. Rich was sent out to run and oversee everything from the staff and what they wore, to what was served on the menus. Once the place was an established success, Rich left and was sent off to open up another location somewhere else. And he still played gigs with his band from time to time—that is, when he wasn't painting artwork that he sold in galleries, or traveling to Italy (he was fluent in Italian, as well as Spanish and Cantonese). And as if he wasn't Renaissance man enough, he now had a total "look" to him. His hair was much shorter and gelled stylishly, he had expensive shoes on, and a Gucci belt rounded out his attire nicely. And he still sported his funky oversized glasses. I admit I'd always liked the glasses.

I was impressed, and as funny as it sounds, I could sense a shift in my feelings about Rich. Aside from when I was scared of Rich my sophomore year, I'd liked him and gotten along with him. He'd always been cool, but there was just something about him now, an intelligent worldliness. And he could definitely pull off wearing a Gucci belt, which is not easy for most straight guys to do. I was attracted to him, and it had nothing really to do with looks; it was everything about him. *How mature of me*, I thought. And then I cursed myself for bringing a date. In fact, I'd all but forgotten about my date, Floppy-Haired Guy. I was sure he was fine, even though he probably had no idea who the cover band, let alone Neil Diamond, was anyway. Marie would look after him.

All of a sudden it was the end of the night. Somewhere along the line, the birthday party had progressed to a bar across the street. The happy and inebriated birthday boy was running around the bar in a crash helmet, taking pictures, and doing shots with people (yes, it was that kind of party), and Rich I were still talking. I hilariously recalled my first so-called conversation with him—my phone call to Dante in which he'd answered, saying, "House of Dildos …" Rich laughed and said drolly, "Ha, yeah, Dante Prosecco. He was cool for about five minutes—the five minutes he dated you."

I was slightly taken aback. Who didn't like Dante Prosecco? Aside from his throwing me over, he was a good guy, yet I decided to take Rich's comment as somewhat of a compliment. I paused, not knowing how to respond. And of course, that was when Floppy- Haired Guy returned. "Hey, ready to go? They're starting to kick people out," he said.

"Oh, okay," I said. Rich and I hugged while Floppy-Haired Guy watched awkwardly. "Nice to meet you, Floppy-Haired Guy," Rich said. "Giuliana, have an awesome time in Italy this summer. I'll make sure Marie gets in a cab home." I waved over my shoulder and left.

The summer came and went fast, and all of a sudden my friend Kit (whom I had shared the apartment with in Italy) and I were planning a Columbus Day party. Yes, I know Columbus Day is no longer considered a politically correct day worthy of celebrating and drunkenly carousing about over—unless, however, you are Italian, like seeing salamis on parade, plan on drinking, or are someone who has the holiday off. I was a yes to all of those, so of course I was going to throw a party. But just so you know, I was in no way celebrating what had happened to the Native

Americans due to Columbus's arrival. This was strictly a "Drink because you're Italian, or even if you're not!" party, quite like St. Patrick's Day or Cinco de Mayo, if you will. It was just a party, folks. Take it easy. We planned the guest list. I decided that Rich Calamari had to be invited. He was Italian. And I wanted to see him. End of story. And before I could even send out the evites, I got an email from Rich inviting me up to the city to some restaurant vendors' party he was attending. Was this kismet? I thought so. But it was on a "school night." It's always been against my better judgment to go out on a school night and up to the city, no less. But I was going. Rich's email was surely a sign. I'd ignored too many signs before, and I didn't want to miss whatever this was.

The vendors' party was at some fancy hotel in the city. It was fun hanging with Rich and watching him scathingly (but humorously) critique all of the food, people, etc. It was just like the olden days when I'd been afraid of him—except now we were both older, and thankfully I wasn't as concerned about him critiquing me. In fact, he was more than chivalrous and kind in regard to myself. I was not opposed.

After making the rounds of the vendors and sampling their foods, we continued the evening in the hotel bar with some other friends who'd come up for the event. When the night was over (and it was really over, since it was two and clearly way past my normal teacher bedtime), I offered to drop Rich off at his hotel, since he said he was going to walk instead of cabbing it. I protested, "Nothing good ever happens after 1:00 a.m., so just let me drop you off. Just to be on the safe side!" He easily agreed.

I pulled up in front of his hotel. "Thanks so much for inviting me. It was really fun," I said.

Rich stared back at me intently, answering, "Yeah, it was. Thanks for making the trek up here on a school night."

Then he leaned in. I could see it coming, like it was in slow motion. And all I could think of was *What is it with me being trapped in the driver's seat with guys?* Not that I wasn't attracted to Rich. But this happening was just putting whatever we were into a whole other category. Even if I'd wanted to escape, there was nowhere for me to go, unless I somehow craftily opened up my driver's side door and fell out into the street. And that would've been weird. So I let Rich kiss me. I think I liked it, but I was still taken aback. He got out, saying he'd call me, and I drove home pondering the randomness of it all and of course whether he would call me.

Rich called me. He also came to my Columbus Day party in North Beach, which was saying something, since he lived in the South Bay. We started seeing each other. And I really liked him, although in some ways I think I still felt a little intimidated by him. He was scary smart and übertalented. But more than that, he made some remarks that had me thinking, *Huh?*

For instance, in one conversation Rich stated in a somewhat patronizing manner, "We'll make a Republican out of you yet!" I was already a Republican. I know, please don't hold that against me. I grew up in a Republican household, okay? It's pretty safe to say that I favor no particular political party anymore these days. But let's not get, well, political. Perhaps Rich didn't intend to sound like he was talking down to me. But I felt like he was playing the all-knowing adult, talking to a silly little girl about what he was going to teach her about what she should be. I didn't like that, and I still don't like that. I have my own opinions. I don't need someone to tell me what they should be. But I shrugged it off because, after all, it was probably just a one-off comment.

And then one day when we were hanging out, that question came up. Rich asked, "So, do you want kids?" It's a valid question for anyone (especially in their midthirties) who's looking to eventually find co-baby making material. Yes, it was a wise idea to ask before proceeding any further.

So I gave what I thought was a plausible, valid, and honest answer. "I don't know." I really didn't. I shrugged. "I obviously love kids, so never say never, but I just … don't know." It wasn't a cop-out answer. Could I have been swayed to have a child if the circumstances were right with the right person? Absolutely. Would I also be okay if that never happened? Yes, I would. Was I going to freeze my eggs or be artificially inseminated? No. And I'm not against that. I have friends who've gone through both processes, and I fully support them. My thought was if having kids was in the cards for me, it would happen. And if it wasn't, that was okay.

Rich whistled and said, "Ooh, wrong answer."

Immediately, a bunch of thoughts swirled in my mind. Why wasn't my answer okay? And who was Rich to tell me that it wasn't? Was he bothered because he'd been thinking of me as a hopeful candidate, or was my answer in general just offensive to him, as if every woman should automatically want children? Did I say any of this out loud? I wish. I'm good with the witty comebacks about five hours after the fact. I was put off, though, and just shrugged. The conversation was basically dead after that exchange, and I left soon after.

Not surprisingly, our short-lived six-week romance immediately started to taper off. Rich had always been busy, but he had now become way too busy to make plans with me. However, he'd frequently check in with me during the week to catch up, but there was no indication he wanted to actually see me. And I didn't bother asking if he'd like to do something. The writing was clearly on the wall. I was kind of disappointed but glad we weren't that far into it. I could get over it. Once I figure out that someone is not interested in me, I like to make a clean break and cut my losses immediately. However, this was a slightly weird situation, since Rich and I had been friends for many years. I couldn't exactly cut him off, and I didn't want to. Yet being the pessimistic Polly I was, I decided to take matters into my own hands. I would be the one to put an end to our wilting relationship. It was clearly going to happen sooner or later anyway. Therefore, I did not want to sit around waiting for Rich to tell me he wasn't interested in dating me any longer.

I planned on saying something the next time we actually talked. Then Rich called me late one night. When I say late, what I mean is it was a half an hour after he knew that I went to bed (which was actually pretty early, but still). I figured he didn't really want to talk to me and was planning on just leaving a message. So, of course, I answered the phone. "Oh! Hey, I didn't think you'd be up," he stammered.

"Surprise," I said. We chatted about this and that for a while. Then, I decided it was time. "So, I was just thinking … you seem really, really busy with work and all. And you and I have been friends for such a long time that maybe it'd be better if we just left it at that. This isn't really working right now," I said.

Rich was quiet a moment and then replied, "Yeah, I know, work has been really crazy lately. But, hey, I still wanna hang out with you."

Cue me rolling my eyes, since we all know that "hang out" really means hook up/make no commitment whatsoever. That wasn't going to work for me, and I was annoyed with him for saying that. "You know, I don't think so. You're really busy. I totally understand. Let's just keep it to being friends."

"Okay, I'll give you a call later on," he said. We hung up. *Whatever.* What was he going to call me about? Yet I was surprised when Rich called me a week later. "Hey, what are you up to this weekend?" he asked.

Okay, for a tiny moment I had that "Yes, he wants to know what I'm doing so he can see if I'm available to go out" thought. And I actually had no real plans. "Not much, what about you?" I said.

He rattled off about ten different things. He was making all the food for the baptism of his friend's baby. He had a family dinner for someone's birthday. Oh, and his band was playing some gig (no, I wasn't invited either), etc. *Yeah.*

"Wow, you've got a busy weekend," I said.

"Oh, God, I know. Well, just wanted to call and say hi."

"Okay, thanks. Talk soon," I answered.

All right, so it was apparent he didn't want to see me, and it was very nice of him to call to say hello. But I didn't get it. Why was he calling to say hello? *Why do guys do that?* If you're not interested, why feign interest? I'd rather you be obvious about showing no interest whatsoever or at least go completely MIA. But don't be confusing. And I was confused, as usual. My guess was that Rich had called just to get a feel as to whether I was pissed off at him. Had he possibly ruined our friendship? I had been very pleasant, though. My niceness and receptiveness to his obligatory call most likely reassured him that I didn't hate him (which I really didn't) and all was okay. Therefore, I wouldn't be hearing from him again, I assumed. And I was right.

A year later, I received an alarming email from our mutual college friend, Tony. Rich had been randomly attacked by some thugs and beaten pretty badly. He was suffering some brain damage and memory loss. Tony asked all of us on the email chain to keep Rich in our prayers. There was also a link to the hospital get-well page to write positive thoughts for Rich. I was completely dumbfounded, as well as horrified by the news. I began to cry as I emailed Tony back. Regardless of our unsuccessful attempt at dating, Rich was a friend whom I cared about.

A few weeks later, Tony asked me if I wanted to go with him and his wife, Kelly, to visit Rich. Tony had been visiting Rich on a regular basis since the attack and had been keeping us all up to date with his progress. "Rich's parents are having an open house for people to come and see him. You should come with us." Tony had called me with this news.

Yes, of course I wanted to go.

I drove with Tony and Kelly to visit Rich at his parents' house. "Okay, so what do we need to know, Tony?" Kelly asked on the drive. "Prep us. Like, is Rich all bandaged up? We need to be mentally prepared so we're not shocked when we see him."

Yes, I was thankful that Kelly had asked what I was wondering myself. I admit I was half expecting to see someone bandaged up like the Elephant Man or something of a horrifying nature like that.

Tony answered, "No, no, Rich looks fine. His injuries are internal. He's got some memory loss. He took a real beating to the head."

I wasn't sure that internal injuries and memory loss sounded any better than the Elephant Man scenario. "Is this going to be weird? Is he even going to know who I am?" I asked, ever bringing the situation back to myself.

"Yeah, will he recognize us?" Kelly asked.

"Girls, he's not blind." Tony laughed.

"Well, you just said he has memory loss, Tony. What do you expect us to think?" Kelly argued.

Once again, I was in agreement with Kelly. Tony responded, "Yes, he has memory loss, but it has to do with other things. Like, he can't remember some words, certain events. He knows people. He totally will know you and remember you."

I was still skeptical. Would Rich recognize me as someone who just looked vaguely familiar, or would he really know and remember me? What if he acted like he was meeting me for the first time? I began to panic slightly, worrying about the complete awkwardness of it all. "Hi, nice to meet you. I'm Giuliana. Yes, we went to college together and recently dated, unsuccessfully, though. Right, yes, I told you I wasn't sure if I wanted kids, and you were unimpressed with that. Ringing a bell yet?" *Oh God. Please let him remember me,* I thought. *And not for just the sake of my pride,* I added hastily. I just couldn't imagine not being able to remember people who'd been a part of your life, no matter how small a part it had been.

At Rich's parents' house, it was all family and close friends. I knew no one except for one of his brothers who I'd met quite a few times during college. We waited our turn in the makeshift receiving line that was occurring as people came up to Rich to say hello. It was surreal, sort of like being at a funeral/wake, with the semihushed talking and the magnificent food spread—except the person was alive and we were conversing with him. I wanted to be there, but I just as much wanted to be about a million miles away. At least Rich still looked the same. Then it was my turn to say hello to him. I waited for the blank look on his face when he wouldn't have a clue as to whom I was. But his face wasn't blank.

"Hey, how *are* you?" He smiled widely and reached out to hug me. Okay, this was good. I inadvertently breathed a sigh of relief, yet I was still waiting for him to suddenly call me some name other than mine, thus proving he had no idea as to my identity. "I'm so glad to see you. How's school?" Okay, he knew who I was, even if he hadn't uttered my name yet. We talked for only a few minutes when Rich said, "Yeah, this is great seeing everyone, but every few minutes I have to go lie down and rest. I get headaches, and it gets a little overwhelming." Out of the corner of my eye, I could see another person waiting to talk to Rich, so I moved aside. Before turning to that person, he said, "Hey, I'll call you later."

My first thought was *What if Rich doesn't really know who I am and has no idea who to call? Or what if he calls someone else, thinking that person is me?* I mean, he had never actually said my name. Maybe he thought I was some other friend who was a teacher. Oh, well. I was still glad I had gone to see Rich.

A few days later, I was having lunch with my friend Jane and debriefing her on the whole Rich attack/memory loss drama. "And then he said he'd call me. What if he doesn't really know who I am? Like he thinks I'm someone else? And why would he want to call me? We aren't dating or anything. I haven't seen him in over a year!" I said plaintively.

Jane replied, "Maybe with the brain damage, he now thinks you're his girlfriend or something. Like, maybe he doesn't remember that you called it quits? God, this is like that show *Samantha Who?* with Christina Applegate! You should really start blogging about your dating life!"

"I wouldn't exactly call it dating," I answered.

"Well, whatever, it's pretty entertaining." Jane laughed.

I had all but forgotten about Rich calling me, when he called a few weeks later. "Giuliana, how are you?"

He does know me. I was glad to hear his voice. We talked for a bit, and I learned he was back in Chicago, working to get some fancy restaurant up and running. He still had memory issues. He could no longer remember any of the recipes he had once known by heart. And every once in a while, he was at a loss to find a word he wanted to say. He came home frequently for brain scans and to check in with doctors. The police were still trying to figure out who had beaten him up and what the motive (if any) had been. But other than that, he sounded pretty good.

"Hey, I want to thank you for coming to visit me at my parents'. That really meant a lot to me."

"Of course," I said. "I am so glad to hear you're doing all right." And I was.

"All right, well, I'll get in touch when I'm back in town sometime." We hung up. It had been great to hear from Rich, but I didn't expect him to call again. Six months later, at the end of December, I got a text from Rich telling me he was in town and to come over to Tony and Kelly's house. He was going to be there with some other college friends. I was excited to catch up with everyone, since the last time I'd seen them all had been when we'd gone to visit Rich.

The evening was good fun. We played beer pong and caught up. And I left Tony and Kelly's with an actual date for New Year's Eve. That was an unexpected turn of events for sure. Rich had asked me to a New Year's Eve party that his cousin was having in the South Bay. "It's a New Year's Eve/We're Glad Rich Is Still Alive party," he told me, chuckling. "I know it's a journey for you, so you can stay at my place so you don't have to worry about drinking and driving. I have tons of space."

Hmm. No, I certainly did not want to deal with drinking and driving on New Year's Eve. Did I want to stay over at Rich's place though? Was this all on a platonic level? Did I want it to be on a platonic level? I wasn't sure, but I'd worry about it later (as in, I'd worry about it on New Year's Eve).

I rang in the New Year kissing Rich. Well, he kissed me, and I admit I kissed him back. Things between us were clearly not platonic. And he would soon be heading back to Chicago to work on the restaurant opening. Leave it to me to get involved with someone who was living out of state. But that was par for the course with me. But then again, I thought I might like it. I was never going to be one of those girls who got sucked into a guy she liked, forsaking all else. I could still have time to myself to do what I wanted. Should we try to pick up with our dating? Yes, this could work, couldn't it? See, every so often, I am very optimistic about things, especially if I believe in them. So yes, I thought so. This could work!

And it did for a little while. For the next couple months, Rich would come home every other week or so to check in with his doctors. We would see each other. He would invite me out; sometimes it would be to things that his family was doing. I didn't mind. However, in the back of my mind I always wondered if it was just a friendship thing between us. But then Rich would get all romantic and hold my hand or kiss me, etc. *I don't do that with my friends.* So, again, my wonderings would be quelled until the next time I saw him.

It was early February, and Rich called me from Chicago. "So, I'd like to take you out to dinner on Valentine's Day. There's a really great Italian place in Los Gatos we should try. Are you available?"

Wait, *what*? The last time I'd been asked to do something on Valentine's Day by someone other than my friends had been when I dated Seamus. And due to the God-awful memories of him, I no longer counted that as Valentine's Day. I was quite shocked. But, uh, yes, I was available. In the week leading up to V-Day, I began to stress. What should I wear? I had no idea what this Los Gatos restaurant was like. Did I buy Rich a gift or just a card, or neither? What did his asking me out for Valentine's Day evening really mean? Per my usual self, I analyzed and overanalyzed those questions to death.

The weekend finally arrived. I'd figured out my wardrobe—dressy jeans, a top, and heels. I'd decided to just get a silly Valentine's card. No need to get ahead of myself with a gift for Rich. And no, I still had no idea what the meaning behind all of this was. I mean, I thought it was safe to assume that someone liked you if he invited you out to dinner for Valentine's Day (and two weeks in advance to boot). And I liked Rich, so I'd leave it at that.

I arrived at Rich's house, and he had a present for me. I know, I know. Normally, I would have fled the scene out of embarrassment for not having a gift to give in return. I'm wired with politeness and etiquette that way. However, Rich's gifts (yes, *gifts*) were not even wrapped. Why? Well, hold onto your seat, because one was a ... plant. Yes, you heard me correctly. No, no, it was not a lovely bouquet of flowers. It was some sort of hearty ... green ... *plant*. Because nothing screams true romance like a ficus, right? Or whatever the hell it was, which I would probably kill in about two days, since I had no green thumb whatsoever. But let's talk about the other gift. It was a chocolate bar. Granted, it was one of those super expensive gourmet chocolate bars, made in Europe, that cost over ten dollars, but really? A plant and a chocolate bar were not gifts for someone from whom you had romantic feelings. They were something you'd give your teacher or grandmother. If there was a theme to these gifts, I'd say it was "Let's be friends."

I realize that I sound like a completely ungrateful, snotty person. Rich didn't have to get me anything. In fact, I wished he hadn't. But that was neither here nor there. "Wow, wow, oh my goodness, thank you," I said, trying my best to sound excited. He gave no explanation for the gifts, like "The reason I got you a plant is because it will last, like my love for you, Giuliana." Okay, well, you get my point. There was just no point to the gifts. I didn't get it and was unsure what I was doing there with Rich. Where were we going with this, with us?

As a result, dinner felt awkward to me. I suddenly had nothing to talk about. And I felt awkward for feeling awkward. We went to a bar after dinner, and I drank vodka sodas, hoping that would spur some interesting conversation. But no. It was unfortunate that I had to stay the night, since I could no longer drive. Again, Rich was all romantic with me. I had no idea why. I'd been given a plant and a candy bar. *Come on.* I didn't see how there could be any romance after that.

When I left the next day, I tried to sneak off without my Valentine spoils, but eagle-eyed Rich noticed and said, "Oh, wait, don't forget your gifts!"

"Oh, yeah, thanks." I smiled weakly. I left completely confused. I liked Rich. However, I was no closer to really knowing how he felt about me, except that he assumed I liked plants and chocolate. It was evident he knew me not. I was kind of annoyed. Should I have been? I don't know, but I was. I bitchily threw the plant out when I got home. But I ate the chocolate, loathing it and myself the whole time.

Two weeks later, Rich was back in town once more to see his doctors. After this visit, he was flying to Venice for his boss's wedding. He called and said he'd like to come up my way to go to dinner. I was excited that he was finally coming to my hood, and I looked forward to taking him to my favorite local Italian restaurant.

The afternoon that Rich was supposed to come up, he called, saying, "Hey, I just got back from my doctor appointment, and we're having a family dinner here. Would you mind coming this way for dinner?"

Yes, I would mind, I thought ungraciously. It was typical that the one time Rich was actually making an effort to come to my neck of the woods, he would cancel. However, I did want to see him before he left for his trip, I didn't want to make him feel badly for having a family dinner, and I had bought him a little gift that I wanted to give him. Therefore, I begrudgingly decided to go.

As I drove through a downpour of rain during rush hour, Rich called and said, "Hey, when you get to my place, call me. We're at an Indian restaurant. From my place, I'll tell you how to get here." All right, there were a few things that were wrong with this scenario. First and foremost, I hate Indian food. And I was starving, so this was a problem. Next, I was navigationally impaired as it was and would now have to find another place in an area with which I wasn't familiar. And, of course, I was going to be even later due to the weather and traffic. I can't stand being late anywhere. To say I was irritated would be a grand understatement. I was close to turning the car around. However, being the good martyr I was, I drove on.

When I reached Rich's, he directed me to the restaurant, which ended up being close by. I breathed a sigh of relief and walked into the restaurant, looking for his large family. And all I spotted was Rich with one cousin. *Wait, family dinner?* I'd been in panic mode about being late and making everyone wait, and it was only Rich and one cousin. Neither Rich nor his one cousin stood up when I got to the table. "Hey, have a seat," Rich said and continued his conversation. I sat there seething in silence for about ten minutes before his cousin offered me something from one of the bowls on the table. "No thanks," I said.

When dinner was over and we walked out, Rich asked, "Hey, wanna drive me back to my place and you can come in for a bit?" *No, I don't want to at all.* But I had his gift in the car, and I did want to give it to him, so I decided I might as well drop him off at least. I'd gotten what I thought was an apropos gift for someone like Rich, going on a trip like this. I bought him two books. One was on the infamous burning of the opera house, La Scala, in Venice, titled *City of Falling Angels*. The other, *The Better Brain*, was all about improving memory and sharpness. Who couldn't use a book like that, especially if you'd had a brain injury, right? Anyway, I thought they'd both sounded like interesting reads and would be good for the flight. I'd even tied them together with a bow.

We got in the car, and I handed the books to Rich, saying, "These are for you, for your trip."

"Oh, thanks," Rich said casually and, without so much as a glance, tossed them onto the dashboard. *Okay.* We drove the short distance to his house, and I pulled into the driveway. Rich grabbed the books, and we both got out and stood by my car. He asked, "Coming in?"

"No," I said, and then I added quickly, "Have a great trip. See ya."

"See ya? Really?" Rich asked with a smirk.

"I guess," I answered shortly.

"Well, okay," he said, and before I knew it, he'd pulled me into a hug. I disentangled myself and got into my car before he could try to kiss me, if he was even going to. On the drive home I cursed myself for going against my better judgment in driving down there and for getting him a gift. What had I been thinking? Apparently, it didn't matter that I'd driven over an hour in a storm to see Rich and that I'd even brought him a gift. But more than that, again, *I didn't matter.*

Rich sent me some lame text the next day in an attempt to be funny. I wrote back with some sort of snarky reply, thinking that that would put an end to the texts. But Rich sent another saying he'd call me when he got back from Venice. *Yeah, right,* I thought. *He'll probably meet someone in Venice.* I rolled my eyes. But whatever the case, I knew I'd eventually be calling him. I had a few things I wanted to say, and by that time I'd have had ample time to collect all my thoughts.

A few weeks passed. When I knew for sure that Rich was back in Chicago, I called and left a message. "Hi, how are you? Just calling to see how your trip was. Give me a call when you get a chance."

Rich called back. We chatted about how lovely his time in Venice had been. "Oh, it was awesome. I hung out with about twenty really cool people who were there for the wedding."

"Oh, how fun." And then I decided to get real. "Can you explain what's going on with us? I feel like there are some really mixed messages I'm getting from you. It's just very confusing. If this isn't going anywhere or whatever, that's fine, but I'd just like to know."

The silence lasted for about three seconds. And then Rich answered, "You know I absolutely love you to death"—ah, here it was, the old proverbial "but" was coming—"but I just don't know, since I'm in Chicago and all. And the funny thing is ... well, um, I met someone in Venice."

Well, of course he fucking met someone in fucking Venice. Besides Paris, wasn't it one of the most (fucking) romantic places in the world? Of course, he had. I couldn't be shocked. I mean, I'd (half) jokingly thought it would happen, hadn't I? Maybe I'd jinxed this or willed it to happen with my silly thoughts. Or perhaps this was God's way of saying, "I needed a laugh today, and this seemed pretty freakin' hilarious."

Whatever the case, I wasn't super-amused. And I wanted to end the conversation pretty swiftly before I lost it.

"Well, great. That's fine, and that's all I needed to know, so now I can move on," I said calmly.

"Look, I still adore you, and I'll call you," he said earnestly.

Ah, yes, the calling again.

"No, don't call me," I said. And then I added, "Well, if you really care about how I'm doing, sure, call me to see how I am. But if you're calling because you feel guilty for being a dick, don't."

"Uh, well, *now* I feel like a dick," Rich answered sheepishly.

"Oh, well. Take care." And I hung up.

Why, why? And why, why Venice? Why couldn't he have been in Iowa? It really didn't matter, I guessed. Look, I knew Rich was not to be the love of my life, but it was still sucky. Again, I felt as if I was just a stepping-stone for another guy to bounce off of to get to his next, better girl. You could like me, but just not enough. When would I be enough?

The Tide Is High

Sometime after Finn and before Rich, Hiro happened. I was living in the city's Sunset District for a hot moment or two. My roomies were none other than one of my best friends, Maggie, and her fiancé, Ryan. Nothing odd about it. The three of us had been hanging out together for years anyway. When Ryan and Maggie got the place in the Sunset, they asked if I wanted to move into the extra bedroom and pay what I thought was a pretty low rent. I was in. I was not worried that moving in would cause our friendship to fall to ruins. As it was, wherever I was living, I was never there the majority of the time. Basically (according to me) that made me the greatest roommate ever. I was tidy, I paid rent on time, and you hardly ever saw me. Yes, the living situation was totally going to work.

The Sunset has typically been a very Irish and Asian San Franciscan enclave. And you can tell just by the names of some of the local bars, like The Dubliner or the Lotus Flower Lounge. Then there are other randoms (people and bars included) such as The Chicken Clucker and Grandpapi's Saloon. I loved it, but of course I had a penchant for the random. And the random usually came in the form of something or *someone* foreign. No matter where I was, I was a magnet for foreigners. Up until then they had always been Irish or possibly Italian. Put me anywhere (a bar, a party, grocery shopping, whatever) and I will somehow meet the only Irish or Italian people (and I mean straight-off-the-plane Irish and Italian) there. I will find them, or they will find me. That's how it was. And now we had Brazilian guys who lived downstairs in the tiny in-law unit. You guessed it—the circle of randomness was about to widen.

Ryan bought a pool table and put it in the garage downstairs. The Brazilians' place was attached to the garage, so we would all frequently conglomerate downstairs at the pool table, having drinks, etc. At one of these impromptu get-togethers, I met Bonnie, who was dating one of the Brazilians. In fact, she was Claudio's fiancée.

Bonnie and I hit it off, possibly due to the copious amount of drinks we had together. That'll bond you, won't it? As a consequence, a few short months later, I was invited to the very small wedding reception for her and Claudio. And when I say small, I mean *small*. It was a block or two away in some friend's miniscule apartment. There were mini quiches and beer and vodka, and not a lot else. But big deal though, because really, wouldn't I be distracted from the heinous food and drink by all the gorgeous Brazilian guys I'd be meeting? I would have had there been any. Pedro, Claudio's hot roommate, wasn't even there, because the two of them couldn't stand each other. That explained all the screaming that we were always hearing from upstairs. Oh, wait, there was one Brazilian guy there. But he had dreadlocks and a wife, so he was out.

And the rest of the guests? They were Lithuanian and Japanese. I'm serious. It was a bizarre mishmash of people from the English language school they all attended. I could've left and probably should've, but I actually had really good hair that night, and I was all dressed up. So, being the trooper I was, I drank, and it was fine. And I met Hiro.

I really don't know how the conversation started. Everyone was getting quite tipsy, and he and his friend began talking to me. The friend was not cute, but Hiro was. He was tall, a bit over six feet, and tan, with these beautiful brownish-gray eyes and long eyelashes. I was a bit mesmerized—and drunk, but more mesmerized. He had on loose jeans, a T-shirt, and flip-flops. While his teeth were gorgeous, they were quite a bit on the grayish side. *Nothing a good supply of Crest Whitestrips can't fix*, I inadvertently thought.

Hiro's accent was thick, but his English was okay—well, much better than his friend, who barely spoke any English. We still hit it off. Hiro had left Toyota, Japan (yes, true city) to travel the world and had ended up visiting some friends who lived in Oakland. Then he'd decided to move across the bay to San Francisco so he could surf every day. Yes, he was a total hardcore surfer. I was liking him even more. He was a carpenter by trade and was taking English because he hoped to return to Japan and open up his own upscale B&B for travelers. We carried on our (limited) conversation on the tiny side patio, since the Lithuanians were starting to get a bit loud. Luckily, Hiro's friend didn't join us.

As our time on the patio progressed, I couldn't tell if the alcohol was helping or hindering our understanding of each other, but it was fun. Besides, don't you know, if someone is not proficient in a language, the best thing to do is to move closer and speak directly into his or her ear? That person will surely understand you then, right? We stood very close and spoke into each other's ears, since we were limited in the conversational language skills and the Lithuanians were being boisterous. And then we were kissing. And just as soon, a fight broke out between the bride and the groom and disrupted the lovely moment.

I have no idea what the fight was about—maybe the fact that the groom had apparently shoved the bride. Why? No one seemed to know, but the consensus was that it was a pretty bad idea and did not bode well for the new marriage. Claudio took off in a Brazilian huff, leaving Bonnie hysterically crying, while friends and family tried to console her.

The rest of us were perplexed as to what to do next. We couldn't really continue the party there, with Bonnie so distraught. How very thoughtful of us. And it was nearing closing time for most bars. One of the Lithuanian guys suggested we (meaning all the females only at the party) go back to his apartment, which was a cab ride away. And he let it be clearly known he had a lot of vodka there. Even in my pickled state, it sounded like a sketchy offer. I did not want to be sold off to the Lithuanian sex slave trade/black market (if there was such a thing), because that would be just my bad luck. I would be the worst sex slave ever, and besides, I was hanging out with Hiro.

I rejected the offer of free vodka, and Hiro and I headed the two blocks to my place. When we got inside, I offered Hiro a drink, because why not keep drinking at two in the morning? He actually declined and suggested (in his broken English) that we go to bed. Before I could even answer, he was declothing himself right in the living room. *Oh.* This probably wouldn't have been that big of a deal, say, if he'd had on boxers. But no. He had no boxers or anything on under his jeans. And now his jeans and the rest of his clothes were lying on the floor. And there he was. No biggie. I stood there, with all my clothes on. I had not been expecting the nakedness quite so soon, or really even at all. I wasn't quite sure where to go with this, except to my room really fast, before either of my roomies happened to walk out.

I guess my face must've given away my surprise, because Hiro explained with a shrug, "I don't wear underwear. When I surf, I don't want to bother with it when I am changing." He said all this with a heavy Japanese accent and broken English, but I got the gist.

"Um, okay! This way!" I whispered while motioning dramatically for Hiro to follow me. I closed the door to my room, and Hiro got into bed. *Okay.* I took off my jacket and shoes and crawled in next to him. In fact, Hiro was lucky I even took off my jacket and shoes. By nature, I am not an exhibitionist, and I also needed some sort of material barrier from him, not that his body wasn't pretty impressive. The barrier was more because it was pretty impressive. And really, it was way too soon for me to deal with any of that, no matter how wasted I was.

The next day, Hiro asked for my number. Despite his no-underwear policy, I liked him, so I gave him my number. He called that week and asked if I'd like to go to dinner. We went to a local sushi place. I tried to adeptly use chopsticks but had trouble breaking them apart. While trying to separate the sticks, one of them boomeranged up out of my hand and onto another table. It was quite embarrassing, not that I wasn't used to embarrassing myself, but even this was taking it to a new level. Hiro laughed in an amused but nice way. I decided to forego the chopsticks.

After dinner, we headed across the street to Grandpapi's Saloon. Over drinks, we got to know each other. I quizzed Hiro about Japan and surfing. Later, somewhat out of the blue, he asked me why I didn't have a boyfriend. Throughout time (or recent dating history), this is typically a question that has two different meanings, one being "Why don't you have a boyfriend? What are you, a big loser?" and the other being "You're such a catch. Why don't you have a boyfriend?" It's a pity one never really knows which meaning is being applied. It would make it a lot easier to answer. For instance, if it were the former, you might say, "I don't have a boyfriend because I'm trying to avoid pathological tools like you," etc.

Anyway, why *didn't* I have a boyfriend? That was a tough one. I was pretty sure (in my most self-deprecating way) that I was a good catch. Sure, I drank a lot, shopped way outside my teacher budget, was superneurotic about my weight, and was fearful of lots of things (including the down escalator at the mall). But I was also a good daughter/granddaughter/sister and a loyal friend, I was well traveled, I could flawlessly open a champagne bottle, and if I liked you in a mushy-gushy way, I would go the distance for you. So, the *good* kind of balanced out the *not so good*, I believed. However, none of that came out of my mouth in reply to Hiro's question.

I shrugged blandly. "I don't know."

Hiro wagged a finger at me and said matter-of-factly, "You don't have a boyfriend, because you don't want one."

"What?" I said in surprise.

But Hiro was off his bar stool. "Smoke," he said, pulling out his pack of American Spirit cigarettes and heading outside.

I sat there, alone with my thoughts. *I didn't have a boyfriend because I didn't want one?* That was silly. Or was it? I always thought I was ready to find love. I'd been open to it many times, hadn't I? But perhaps I did subconsciously keep real love at bay. Seamus had pretty much ruined my ability to put complete trust in someone else. But I'd assumed I'd moved on from the trauma. I mean, Seamus barely even came to mind anymore at all, unless someone had the bad misfortune of mentioning him in conversation. Maybe Hiro was right. How had he seen it, when even I hadn't seen it? I could only drink so much alcohol to achieve the effect of being receptive and ready for love. And at that point, I wasn't sure how much I could drink … but the drinking didn't seem so bad, though.

What I wasn't really aware of yet, at this time, was that my drinking was a shield, a huge cover-up for feeling anything real. Because real was scary. I didn't like being scared, and I was a worrier by nature. Alcohol was sneakily becoming my security blanket in all my romantic scenarios. So, I didn't have a boyfriend. So, I couldn't seem to keep a guy around long enough. Was that my fault? I was the victim, the one constantly wronged, wasn't I? That's what I thought. But back to Hiro.

If you asked me, compared to the guys I dated, I had no problems whatsoever in my life. While Hiro appeared to be a happy-go-lucky surfer dude who enjoyed surfing (duh) and smoking pot (double duh), and drinking beer, and not necessarily in that order, there was a darker, sad side to him. He had grown up with a very abusive father. His only brother had committed suicide. Hiro hated to leave his mother with his father but decided he had to escape the toxicity and sadness of his home life. He'd been traveling the world and surfing—from Israel to Bali and all over Europe, and now in California. And here I was on another night, sitting across from him at the Beach Chalet and listening to his story. What do you say to any of that? Sure, my parents had split up when I was six, but in the grand scheme of things, I seemed okay. In fact, I seemed perfectly fine. I felt I'd somehow gotten lucky compared to Hiro.

And of course, his trauma endeared him even more to me. No, I didn't like trauma, per se. But I just knew he needed someone like me. And I wanted someone to need me. I mean, if anyone is in need of being taken care of or listened to, or has been exploited, whatever, I'm your girl. That much was clear. I was like that kid out finding stray puppies and bringing them home (much to the chagrin of the family). I was a nurturer and a sucker for cute puppies (or in this case, boys). Yes, I was going to be the girl who would save this poor unfortunate soul, Hiro.

Yeah, things didn't work out as I'd planned. I'm sure you're surprised. I was. As much fun as it was dating Hiro—what with him and his pocket dictionary and notebook he'd constantly carry around to write down sayings I'd throw out and what they meant (see, I *was* helping him with his English)—it just wasn't going anywhere. At least, it wasn't going where I wanted it to go, since I do like to direct things.

We'd been seeing each other for at least four months, and Hiro had yet to even invite me over to his apartment (or room he rented), which was only a few blocks away. Weird, right? I got the feeling he was embarrassed about it, but he'd never really say. He preferred coming over to my place. He'd even bought sweats and other odds and ends that he could leave with me. That had to mean something, I thought. Or it meant he really just didn't want me coming over.

And if ever questioned (by me, of course) about whether I was his girlfriend (yes, I wanted to know), he was always very vague. I had a problem with that. Hiro did not. He was not one to rock the boat either way. He'd laugh and ask why I wanted to know. Well, why wouldn't I want to know? Was this a cultural thing? Was this a surfer/pothead thing? Or was this a guy who's not into you thing? In hindsight, I'd say it was a little of each. However, I let myself remain annoyed and confused for a little while longer—that is, until Hiro's "yoga friend" came to town.

I do not know her name. It wasn't even clear if Hiro knew her name. He only referred to her as his "yoga friend." I really wanted to be bitchy and correct him by saying, "You mean *your friend* that you *met taking yoga*?" but I didn't. The sarcasm would've been lost in translation. So, yoga friend was in town for the weekend. Hiro was going to see her and hang out with her. And I was not invited to meet her. Therefore, according to me, we were now over. Because I knew, I just knew, they were not getting together to reminisce about their yoga days. Call it a woman's intuition, call it jealous paranoia, call it he's a total noncommittal stoner, call it whatever—I was calling it quits. Hiro didn't know I was calling it quits, but I didn't think he'd be too upset anyway, if he ever figured it out.

I was packing up boxes one Saturday a month later. I'd decided to move out of the apartment. Maggie and Ryan had just gotten married. Although they'd already been together for years and swore they wanted me to stay, I'd decided to let them be newlyweds. It was time for me to go. I came across Hiro's T-shirts and sweats. I called him up. "Hey, your stuff is here. Do you want me to just leave it in a bag for you by the front door?"

"No, that's okay. You can just throw it all out," he answered. Throw it out? Clearly, no attachment there.

"How are you?" Hiro asked in his thick accent.

"Great, busy," I answered as I schlepped a box downstairs and out to my car, my phone pressed between my head and shoulder. I was secretly enjoying the fact that he had no idea I was moving out, literally, as we were speaking. And I wasn't about to tell Hiro, because I knew he wouldn't care. Nothing was a big deal to him. Of course, that was probably because he was stoned a lot of the time and drank heavily, but whatever.

He began talking, and I immediately cut him off, saying, "Okay, well, talk to you later." And I hung up. We'd never talk again. I threw Hiro's clothes in the garbage and lugged another packing box downstairs.

"It Is What It Is and What Not."

It was becoming more and more apparent (if not to myself, then at least to everyone else) that I was the poster child for someone who would attract and, yes, date dysfunctional males. Send me your poor, emotionally and geographically unavailable, huddled masses, yearning for credit or codependency, or just yearning to break free (probably from prison) … yes, send them to me, and I will pick up the pieces or end up in pieces trying to do so. Why this had become the norm for me, I still had yet to figure out. And … next!

My grammar school friend, Frankie, was in town for a weekend with his girlfriend. Another group of his friends was going out in downtown Burlington, and he invited me along so we could catch up and I could meet the new girlfriend. I showed up at the restaurant, and everyone was already hanging around the bar, drinking wine. It was clear I had some catching up to do. Aside from Frankie, I didn't know anyone, since they'd all gone to various local public high schools. And since we all know that I didn't frequent any high school ragers, none of our paths had really crossed before.

Frankie, in his socializing element, chatted with everyone else and left his girlfriend, Holly, and me to bond. She obviously didn't know anyone either, so it was a good fit. We got along great, drank wine, and swapped Frankie stories. There was a guy in the group of people sitting at the other end of the table. He was a brooding sort, seemingly unimpressed with everyone, and dressed in black jeans and a black button-up. I wasn't necessarily opposed to the Johnny Cash look. I, myself, wear black all the time. Come on, it's slimming. Anyway, looks-wise, he was a cross between ex-football player Junior Seau and Sylvester Stallone. I wasn't opposed to that either. He seemed pretty tight with one of the girls in the group, and I just assumed they were together. I didn't think much of it, since no one seemed too interested in talking to Holly and me anyway.

After a while, it was somehow decided that we were heading to a bar two doors down. It was a bar my friends and I never frequented, because it was known to be a haven for drug dealers and other sketchy types. When you've had a few glasses of wine though, you're game for anything. Besides, this was Burlington (a.k.a. J.Crew Suburbia Central). How dangerous could the potential drug dealers be? They'd probably be wearing seersucker and flip-flops. Not exactly scary, I reasoned with myself. It was there, while ordering the first of many vodka sodas, that he introduced himself to me.

"Hey, I'm Ray. We didn't get introduced at the restaurant." He stuck out his hand to shake.

"Hi, I'm Giuliana. I'm a friend of Frankie's. I think he just assumes everyone pretty much knows everyone already," I said, taking a hold of his big hand.

"I guess." Ray laughed. "I'm a good friend of Tessa. We've known each other since high school. I met Frankie through her. Tessa called and said she and Greg were meeting up with Frankie and everyone tonight, so I came down from the city."

"Who's Greg?" I asked. I really had no clue as to whom I was hanging out with.

"Greg is Tessa's boyfriend. That one." He nodded in the direction of Tessa and a blond-haired guy.

Huh. Ray wasn't with Tessa. *Huh.* It was on. Ray and me. Everyone else just seemed to fade into the background, including Frankie and Holly, who watched amusedly from the sidelines. We continued our marathon of Ketel One and sodas from the drug-dealer bar to another bar that had dancing. *Oh, boy.* Ketel One and soda, a dance floor, and me—watch out. And everybody did watch, believe me.

"*Shawty had them Apple Bottom jeans (jeans), boots with the fur (with the fur) ...*" Flo Rida pumped as we danced while trying not to spill our drinks on each other. It was next to impossible, but we got an A for effort. And of course, why not try to carry on an in-depth conversation, with Flo Rida shouting, as well? It totally made sense.

"She hit the floor (she hit the floor). Next thing you know Shawty got low low low low low low low low," the song played on as Ray and I tried shouting in each other's ears as our drinks sloshed.

This, of course, led to an inevitable make-out session on the dance floor that I am shamefully mortified about still.

When Lady Gaga's "Bad Romance" began blaring, we unattached ourselves and walked off the dance floor. The song should've been an indication of what was to come for the next nine months or so. However, my dating intuition was impaired at that point, and we proceeded to leave together. Ray offered to drive me home, which was actually a horrible idea given the imbibing we'd done. But sure, why not? It was a short drive from Burlington to the next town, where I lived, I reasoned. We got to Ray's car, and I inadvertently shuddered. "What's the matter? Second thoughts?" he asked with a laugh.

Actually, yes, I thought. *Funny how fast you can sober up.*

He drove a *silver Mercedes CLA-Class.* I had momentary flashbacks to Seamus and the heinous car debacle. The only thing that actually made Ray's car worse was the fact that it was a convertible. Well, I was sure that, given the chance, Seamus would've driven some type of convertible. I tried not to gag.

"Oh. Nothing. My ex-boyfriend had this exact same car."

"Fond memories?" Ray joked, raising his eyebrows.

"Was a long time ago, and that's all I'm going to say." I smiled.

"Shall we?" He held the door open for me, and I slid in. We made it safely into my neighborhood. I had Ray park slightly past the driveway. I had obviously told him that I lived at my grandmother's, and it hadn't seemed to put him off. I wondered what was wrong with him. *Never mind,* I thought. But still, I was not keen on Grandma finding out about Ray, so parking in the driveway was a no-go. Grandma's lights were off in her bedroom, but I could see that the kitchen light was on. Now I just had to worry about my other roommate, Grandma's beagle.

Sadie, with her eagle-beagle ears, was out the doggie door before I could even unlock the back door to the kitchen. "Ray, Sadie. Sadie, Ray," I introduced them while giving Sadie a scratch behind the ear.

"Hey, girl." Ray bent over to pet Sadie. "I have a dog too," he said.

"Oh, what kind?" I asked. What kind of dog could he have living in an apartment in the city?

"A Chihuahua," Ray answered. That answered my question. I never would've pegged this stocky Soprano-looking guy to be the owner of a Chihuahua, but Ray hadn't struck me as the convertible-driving type either. He was certainly throwing my assumptions and me for a loop.

We left Sadie in the kitchen and walked to the back of the darkened house. "Grandma's not going to wake up and freak out, is she?" Ray whispered.

"Her light's out and so are her hearing aids, so I doubt it."

We made it safely past Grandma's closed door and into my room at the very back of the house. I breathed a small sigh of relief and then wondered what the hell I was doing bringing a guy to Grandma's. I'd done a lot of dumb things under the influence, but really? However, the thought fleetingly passed, and I left Ray on my bed as I went to wash my face and brush my teeth. I sincerely hoped Ray didn't pull a Hiro on me. *Please let him have clothes on when I come out*, I prayed.

My prayer was answered. I came out of the bathroom and found Ray passed out (fully clothed) on top of the bed and looking very corpse-like, I might add. His hands were folded on top of his chest. *And please don't let him be dead either*, I suddenly thought in a slight panic. No, he wasn't dead. I could see his chest rise and fall slightly. I changed into some sweats and passed out next to him.

Ray's alarm on his phone went off, and we both woke up. It was six in the morning. Ray did IT work for a software company and was on duty that morning. As Ray got his shoes on, I peeked out the bedroom door. Grandma's bedroom door was open. That meant she was up and in the kitchen. I had to get Ray out fast through the front door. Cue *Mission Impossible* music as I grabbed Ray's hand and tried to quickly usher him out.

The front door was in an alcove off the living room. The swinging door from the dining room into the kitchen was closed. So far so good.

"So, can I get your number?" Ray pulled out his phone.

"Yes, sure." I rattled off my number.

And then I heard the door to the kitchen open and Grandma say, "Giuliana?"

We both froze, and Ray's eyes bugged out. I waited and hoped that Grandma would go back into the kitchen.

"Giuliana? Are you out here?"

Oh, shit. "Go in there!" I quickly pointed to the door next to the front door that led to what we called the powder room.

"What?" Ray whispered in a panic.

"*There*, go in *there!*" I shoved him in, closed the door, and jumped out of the alcove.

"Morning," I said as I walked into the living room.

Grandma was standing in the dining room in her flannel blue robe. "Oh, there you are. I thought I heard something." She smiled.

What? Right, of course her hearing aids decided to work this morning at six.

"I was just going to check if the paper was on the front walk," I said, my heart pounding. "I'll get it and bring it in." I backed away toward the front door.

"Okay, thank you," Grandma said. I waited until she'd gone back into the kitchen.

I opened the bathroom door and laughed at Ray standing there in the dark.

"Oh my God, I almost had a heart attack!" he hissed, shaking his head.

"Sorry about that. We better get you out of here fast in case she decides to come back out. Uh, don't walk across the driveway. Just go down the walkway and to the street."

"Got it, okay. Call you later." He kissed me good-bye and practically sprinted down the front walkway and out to his car. I ran out, got the paper, and closed the front door.

Our first date happened the following week. We met at an Italian restaurant in Burlington. Dinner conversation consisted of repeating whatever we'd discussed the night we met, since my drinking amnesia prevented me from remembering anything of importance. Ray had gone to a local public high school and junior college, where he'd played baseball. Then he'd gone to a state college. He'd been living and working in the city for a while. Yes, it was all coming back to me.

Oh, and Ray was even more interesting than I'd remembered. His background was very colorful. He had never met his real father, who'd abandoned the family after Ray was born. His mother later remarried and had his half-brother. His stepfather was in the army, and the family had lived in Spain for quite a while. When his mother and stepfather split, they moved back to the States. During high school, he moved out and into an apartment by himself. "Really?" I asked. "How did you pay rent?"

"I had money." Ray smiled. *What the hell?* I thought. However, I always went for the independent/lone wolf type, didn't I? I smelled dysfunction, and I liked it. I was all about the underdog, since I usually felt like one myself. When I asked Ray about his brother, he said, "Oh, well, he was incarcerated for a while."

"Oh," I said lightly, as if I talked about incarcerated brothers all the time. Anyway, I wasn't about to pass judgment on Ray because his brother had been in prison. I wanted to know why but couldn't bring myself to ask. I didn't have to, though.

Ray went on, saying, "Yeah, my brother didn't get along with our dad. He got kind of physical with my brother, and my brother couldn't take it and got a little out of hand. Well, then the whole thing kind of got blown out of proportion by my stepmom. She had my brother arrested for attempted murder."

Obviously. There's not much you can say in response to a statement like that, is there? I mean, I had no attempted murder/incarceration stories of my own to share, thank God. Ray then shared about the breakup of him and his ex-girlfriend. They'd dated/lived together for four years and had a dog together (yes, the aforementioned Chihuahua).

"What happened?" I asked.

"She really drank a lot, and it became a relationship where I was always having to look out for her, like a babysitter. I couldn't deal with it anymore."

I nodded my head in understanding as I took a large swig of my pinot grigio. If my foggy memory served me right, Ray was quite a drinker, as well. So for him to end it with someone because she drank too much ... well, I figured the girl must've had a *serious* drinking problem. However, that wasn't going to rain on my pinot grigio parade.

"So, what's your story? You must have some ex-boyfriend stories."

Oh, Jesus. Why did he have to ask that? Of course I did, but that was the last thing I wanted to talk about. I mean, if I told Ray about all my ridiculous dating scenarios, he'd take me for some kind of freak magnet (which I was). Or I would sound like some bitter, jaded person (which I was possibly starting to become).

Before I could object to the ex-boyfriend topic, Ray said, "Aw, come on, you must have some. I told you mine." He smiled and took a sip of his drink.

I dislike being goaded into divulging personal information way too soon, just because someone else has. And really, who needed to know I was embarrassingly a failure with guys?

"Come on, *come on*," Ray said again.

Fine, I thought. I had a story that would shut him up and probably cause him to flee the restaurant. I then shared the shortened, two-minute version of the Seamus-take-back-the-car story.

When I was finished talking, Ray whistled and then said, "*Damn*, girl, you are one badass!" I shrugged. He then added with a smile, "I like that. And don't worry, I own my Mercedes."

"Oh, good. I like *that*," I said and laughed. *Phew.* From then on out, it was smooth sailing. Ray and I got along great. For some reason, he thought I was hilarious and was my greatest audience of one. I was somehow able to be myself around him. It was different this time. Even though I was enamored of him and his own badass ways, I was never uncomfortable just being me. This was a lovely turn of events, I thought. And then, naturally, a month or so in, Ray went missing because ... well, because he was a guy, and I happened to be dating him. That's usually how it worked thus far.

I was hanging out at my friend Jane's and was relating the Ray-missing-person scenario to her and her husband, Dan.

"When was the last time you heard from him?" Jane asked.

I thought a moment and then answered, "We were texting back and forth yesterday and the day before. He asked what I was up to over the weekend. I really hate that question. What does it mean anyway?"

"Doesn't it mean 'What are you doing over the weekend'?" Dan interjected with a laugh.

Jane and I both looked at him with pity and shook our heads. "No, no, not necessarily. It could mean 'What are you doing, because I want to know so I can possibly ask you out if you're not busy?' Or it can just mean you're being polite, trying to make conversation, like 'Oh, what are you up to?'" I said and then added, "Which is a problem, because you then don't know how to answer. Like, do I say I have nothing going on in hopes that he'll ask me out? Or am I going to look like a loser because I have no plans, and now he hasn't asked me out anyway?"

"Ah, yes, I see," Dan said and then shook his head. "God, you girls are so complicated."

"Well, how did you answer?" Jane said, ignoring Dan.

"I said I had lunch plans with friends today (true), and then I asked what he was doing this weekend. And I never heard back from him."

"You asked him a specific question and no response? Weird," Jane said.

"How hard is it to answer a question? Make something up. I don't care. And what is the point of even texting someone if you're not interested in them? Clearly, that's the case here, right?" I said.

Jane looked at Dan and said, "Dan? Thoughts? Let's get a male perspective."

Dan looked up from the book he was reading. "Hmm, don't rule him out yet. Okay, he didn't answer, but he could've gotten distracted or been busy. Maybe he had other plans over the weekend. It's only been a day, right? If you reach the seventy-two-hour mark and no word, then it's most likely over."

"I'm sure you'll hear from him," Jane said hopefully.

I did hold some feeble hope. The seventy-two-hour mark came and went, and there was no word from Ray. I couldn't say I was surprised, but I was disappointed. I decided there would definitely be no reaching out on my part.

Two months later, on New Year's Day (well, 1:00 a.m. specifically), a text came through from Ray. "Happy New Years bitchezzzz!" Insert drunk-looking emoji. *Hmm.* I wasn't a bitch, and not in the plural form, unless I was really pissed off. This was definitely a group text, no doubt sent to anyone who was in Ray's phone contacts.

My first thought, besides being annoyed by the incorrect spelling, was to think that it was beneath me and unworthy of a text reply. As usual, I ignored my gut instinct. I waited until a decent hour the next day to respond.

I wrote, "I prefer to be referred to as beautiful instead of bitch. Happy New Year."

I received a speedy response back. "Happy New Year, Beautiful." Heart emojis were everywhere. And then he sent another text: "What are you doing tomorrow night?" Before I could get further annoyed by the question, another text came in telling me to come to some guy's birthday party at some bar in Burlington. I'd already been invited to the party by Ray's friend Tessa. I had been on the fence about going, but now, however, I decided I'd make an appearance.

I showed up later than I normally would and sat at a table with Tessa and friends. Ray turned around from where he was at the bar and spotted me. A smile came over his face, and he sauntered over. "Hey, happy New Year." He gave me a hug and a kiss.

"What have you been up to?" he asked.

"Christmas vacation. I go back on Monday," I answered.

"Oh, that's right. Man, I've been so busy. They changed my work schedule, so now I'm working nights 10:00 p.m. to 6:00 a.m."

"Eww, that's horrible," I said, and I meant it. "What days do you have off?"

"Thursday and Sunday," Ray answered. I winced.

"Rough," I said.

"Yeah, I know. Sorry I haven't been in touch."

I doubted his new schedule was the reason I hadn't heard from him, since I'd "happened" to spot some skanky girl (yes, I Facebook stalked, I'm ashamed to say) posting x's, o's, and smiley faces on his Facebook wall lately, but whatever. We'd see what happened next.

Things progressed again. I heard from Ray on a regular basis, despite his weird work hours. He even invited me up to the city for Valentine's Day. I hoped I wouldn't be the recipient of another plant and gourmet candy bar. I opted to not get Ray anything but instead brought a bottle of Veuve Clicquot, which was really a gift for myself. At the very least, I'd be drinking half of it anyway.

I needn't have worried about receiving a horrible gift; Ray wasn't that thoughtful. There was no gift, but I was okay with that. Were we in a relationship? I guessed it was some sort of relationship. I wasn't seeing anybody else, and I didn't want to. I was in total like with Ray. With Ray's work schedule, I doubted he'd be able to see anyone else, but who knew? As of now, all was still well.

Before you knew it, the three-day Presidents' Day weekend was approaching. Since Ray had Sunday off, I invited him to come over for dinner. I'd make dinner, and maybe we'd go out afterward.

"Sounds great, I'll be there," he texted.

That Sunday morning, I sent Ray a text letting him know what time to show up. I didn't hear anything but didn't think too much of it. It was his day off. He was probably sleeping in and then running errands. Late afternoon rolled around, and still there was no text. I was a little anxious but did nothing. I prided myself on not being one of those nagging female types. He'd show—at least, I hoped so.

When seven thirty rolled around and there was no sign of, nor text from, Ray, I sent him a text. The food I'd cooked would be cold but could be salvaged and heated up, should he still arrive. However, I was not that dumb. I knew he wasn't coming, and I was baffled. No word all day. Even if he'd decided to bail, couldn't he have made something up and sent a message?

As nine o'clock arrived and still nothing from Ray, I wrapped up all the uneaten food and stuck it in the fridge. I poured myself another glass of prosecco and fumed. I was beyond irritated. Who accepted a dinner invitation and then blew it off without even a word of explanation? *Assholes, that's who.* Forget about texting. I was going to actually call him on his cell. I wanted an answer of some sort.

I dialed, and after a few rings, his voicemail came on asking me to leave a message. Oh, I was going to.

"Ray, hi. Not sure what's going on with you or where you are. Really hope you're not in a ditch somewhere. Call me."

Not my finest phone message, I'll admit. However, I doubted I'd hear from Ray anyway. I went back to fuming and my bottle of prosecco, and called it a night.

I woke up the next morning slightly hungover and still totally annoyed. I went about my day off: I worked out, went to coffee with friends, and let some steam off to them about the dinner-ditching situation. Everyone thought it was bizarre and, of course, very rude. I could do better, everyone thought, and I had to agree.

I lamented (to myself) that in regard to the caliber of guys I'd been involved with thus far, the bar wasn't exactly set high. In fact, it was pretty near being on the floor ready to trip me. If I liked you (and let's be clear, there had to be some sort of redeeming qualities there), I'd be willing to give you the benefit of the doubt. You didn't have to be perfect, really. But honesty was a must. And if you couldn't be honest, at least send a lame-ass excuse telling me you were in a car accident, making a dinner date impossible. I'd like you a lot less, but at least I'd know something.

And … he was in a car accident. *Holy hell.* What were the odds? I got home from my coffee date with friends and noticed I'd missed a message from Ray, since my phone had been in my purse. I listened to Ray speak in a superslow, groggy voice. "Hey, Giuliana, I was in a car accident yesterday. Got sideswiped. I'm in the hospital, and they have me on morphine. Sorry about not making it to dinner. I'll call you later." *Click.*

Aside from being shocked, I now felt like an ass for leaving a snarky message about him being in a ditch. Let's be frank, when I said I hoped he wasn't in a ditch, what I really meant was that he *better* be in a ditch to not have called me about missing dinner. Of course, I didn't really want him to be in a ditch or, in this case, a car accident. *Oh God, have I thrown bad energy out into the world?* No, no. I wasn't that powerful. As much as I liked to be in control of things, I didn't think I was capable of accidentally using the Jedi mind trick to cause car accidents. *Phew.* That was a relief.

And then my inner Florence Nightingale kicked in. *What can I do? Does he need me? How can I help? Should I go visit?* Well, that's what I was, a helper. Let's not forget, when the chips were down, I was always going to be there. Ray's chips were definitely down now. I could be his rock, couldn't I? So noble, right? Yes, gag away, but that's what I thought.

Ray was a mess, with some cracked ribs, a broken collarbone, a broken wrist, and bruises all over. The doctor stated he was lucky to be alive. As much as I would've liked Ray's crash to have brought us closer together, it rather succeeded in only making me feel as if I was just another friend—nothing wrong with that, unless you're supposedly in a dating relationship. I really wanted to be in all my Florence Nightingale glory, but alas, I was only one of the many who were helping Ray out by bringing food and groceries, and visiting. I don't think I ever even saw him alone in his injured, pain-medicated state. There was always some coworker or friend who was around helping out. My nursing abilities were definitely foiled.

Ray recovered, no real thanks to my help. Due to his work schedule, we saw each other sporadically. I got a bit tired of never actually seeing him but instead seeing his many, *many* Facebook posts. Ray was definitely an overposter. Either he'd post some very funny one-liner or inspirational quote, or he'd resort to cryptic posting. You know those people who are cryptic posters. The people who post just enough to let you know something's horribly wrong in their lives so they get attention and comments. It's so very annoying. Don't be all coy and mysterious, because you're really not being all that mysterious. But I digress.

So, Ray was in cryptic-poster mode. His post popped up one morning on my Facebook feed. It read, "Why does life suck so much? Why do people have to suffer?" Sad, teary emojis emphasized that life sucked and people had to suffer.

Naturally, I was worried. What had happened? I scrolled down the comments to see what was up.

"Ray, hope all is all right with you."

"Man, I'm here for you."

"Life will get better! We love you!"

"If you need anything just call anytime" (smiley face and heart emojis from the Facebook skank).

And so on and so on. I kept scrolling down, looking for answers to the comments. Now I was really worried. What the hell had happened, and why didn't I know about it? I'd been seeing him (albeit sporadically at times) for the past nine months. Why hadn't he called me? Finally, there was a reply to one of the comments from Ray, saying he'd just found out that an uncle of his in Texas had cancer. I believe it was an uncle whom he'd told me he hadn't seen or really talked to in over twenty years—not that it mattered, of course.

I realize that people react very differently to painful news. Some people share important/sad/happy news with their loved ones and close friends. Some don't share it at all. And then there are some people who'd rather tell their six-hundred-plus Facebook friends the news before they tell people they're actually supposed to be in relationships with. But who was I to judge? No one, but I still got judgy. I rolled my eyes with disdain. *Oh, please,* I thought. I felt completely horrible that his uncle had cancer. I really did. However, I just didn't get Ray and his cry for attention from Facebookers.

I felt like commenting with one of Ray's favorite (and in my opinion annoying) sayings: "It is what it is and what not." It didn't matter what we were discussing, but Ray would always drop in an "It is what it is and what not" at the end of a sentence. Sometimes I knew what *it* was, but most of the time I felt that *it* in general was very elusive—just a filler. Anyway, no, I did not comment with an "It is what it is and what not." I'm not always that bitchy.

Instead, I called Ray and left a message saying I hoped he was all right and that I'd seen the Facebook post and was sorry to hear about his uncle. I asked him to call me when he got the chance. I received no word from him. I guessed he was too distraught, although he kept posting shit on Facebook about feeling sad. I read the posts and all the comments but didn't comment myself.

Why would I? I'd already called him and left a message. I wanted to actually talk to him or even see him in person. Enough of the social media crap! Enough of the texting! I was a real person, someone who cared, and I was there all the time if Ray needed someone to talk to. But he obviously preferred Facebook friends and the fact that you could receive scads of attention while keeping people at an arm's distance. In other words, no real commitment was necessary.

One night I was drinking prosecco (no shocker there) with my friend Bella at my favorite Italian restaurant. Bella knew Ray, because, unlike me, she'd gone to public high school and had hung out in the same crowd as him. And Bella (God bless her) was always quick to remind me how ridiculous Ray behaved.

"Why the hell does he post shit like that? What's with the 'Oh, poor me' crap? And where the hell has he been? What the fuck is his problem? I can't believe he just leaves you hanging like that!"

Well, I had to agree with her. No, Bella was not easily impressed, and Ray clearly didn't impress her at all. I admitted to myself that I was no longer impressed either.

"Gimme your phone. I wanna see his Facebook page again and his stupid posts! I really should block him. I get so annoyed," Bella said, swiping my phone out of my hand.

She scanned my phone and then asked, "What is HotLove.com?"

"I don't know." I shrugged. "Why?"

Bella answered, "He's got all these posts on his page … 'Ray likes Hot Cakes 408 on HotLove.' 'Ray likes HotGUrlGIGI on HotLove.' Oh, and here's a good one, 'Ray likes Bambigoestwerking on HotLove.' It goes on and on. What the hell?"

"Let me see that." I snatched the phone away from Bella.

It appeared that HotLove.com was some dating site. And it appeared that Ray was on it. It also appeared that he was a bozo and hadn't hit the privacy button that disallowed his HotLove favorites to appear on his Facebook page.

"Oh God," I said with disgust.

"Yeah, he's real distraught over that uncle of his. He can't text or call you back, but he's got enough time for HotLove!" Bella cackled.

"I think it's time to defriend. I don't want to be looking at that or have that pop up on my feed," I said.

"You can just block him," Bella said.

"I'm done. I've been there for him, and he'd rather be in touch with Hot Cakes 408? Nope. I'm going to text him right now and end this."

Bella replied, "Is this the prosecco talking, or do you really want to do this?"

"Prosecco has nothing to do with this," I answered. It really didn't, but it also didn't hurt either. Texting was tacky, but I felt Ray had already stepped over the threshold of tackiness by striking it up with Bambigoestwerking and company on HotLove.com. Defriended. Done. I drafted a text that read, "Hi Ray, I've heard nothing from you, yet you continue to share your (apparently) darkest moments with all of Facebook. The fact that I have to text this is ridiculous. I think it's time we go our separate ways. I deserve better treatment."

Bella looked over the text and nodded. "Okay."

Before she could say anything else, I grabbed the phone and hit "Send."

Bella laughed. "I was going to ask if there's anything else you want to add, but all right!"

I took a sip of my prosecco and added, "I probably won't even hear from him anyway." And with that my phone buzzed right in front of me. I looked down at it, startled.

"Stop, is that him?" Bella shouted.

"Yes, of course it is. This should be a good one." I read his text.

"Giuliana, hi. Yes, you are much too good for me and deserve better. I'm really sorry about this, but I guess it is what it is. Ray."

I snorted and rolled my eyes. It was what it was and what not.

"You Say Potato. I Say ... Spuds."

So there I was, in the midst of my lunch break, correcting second-grade picture vocabulary, when my phone, which had been sitting on the table so I could easily glance at the time every so often, vibrated. *Ah, it's from Connor.* My heart skipped just a tad. Connor was an Irish guy (I know, I know, another Irish guy), a very cute Irish guy who'd taken to texting me as of late. Having an assortment of Irish friends and being out with some of them one night, I happened to run into him ... why, yes, in a local Irish bar. It was a night like any other in an Irish hole-in-the-wall dive bar. At least I am assuming.

I'd sauntered into O'Hooley's with one of my BFFs, Maggie. We'd come from an amateur boxing tournament in San Francisco that Maggie and her husband had actually organized and put together. Therefore, by the time it was all over and we hit O'Hooley's, it was close to, if not a bit after, midnight.

Now, the odds of meeting anyone worthwhile after midnight in O'Hooley's runs the gamut: either slim to none (unless you're into odd men with Beatles hairdos or drinking problems who blatantly stare at you while standing inordinately close so as to violate the whole personal space requirement), or quite excellent (if you're into the previously mentioned men or if for some reason attractive younger men happen to accidentally stumble in to have a few drinks and never leave). That said, go in with *no* expectations whatsoever, and you won't be disappointed. You may even be pleasantly surprised, as I was to be later on.

But to be sure and with all due respect to this drinking establishment, clearly the best time to pay a visit is when everyone in the place has had quite a few cocktails, as you will appear most alluring, fresh-faced, and attractive compared to all the other boozers who've been drinking their bloated faces off the entire evening.

While this can work to one's advantage, it can also be quite troublesome if the bar patrons are especially freaky and aggressive with their liquid courage, which is why you must wait to enter this type of bar (with friends, *always* with friends) after others have been drinking awhile and after you've had, at the very least, a couple of adult beverages yourself. Then nobody appears quite so scary. They're just weird and annoying but not as likely to send you running out the door.

But I digress. So, we'd had a couple (in addition to the couple we'd had earlier at the fights) and were standing at the end of the bar, chatting with some other folks, when I noticed at the other length of the dimly lit bar someone approaching and, if I may say so, making an actual beeline for me. And he was good-looking too. Yes, it was him, Connor, of the latter rain slicker text.

"Hello, Giuliana, how are ya?" he said in his cheerful Irish brogue, Corona with lime in hand.

"Hello, Connor. Great, and you?" I answered, as if seeing a long-lost friend.

Now here's the weird part. We didn't actually know each other at all. In fact, I don't know if I'd ever even met him. But I knew who he was. Years before, at another Irish function (or bar, or function *at* a bar), I'd spotted him and inquired about him. See, I'd thought he was cute back then too but heard he'd had a girlfriend and also guessed him to be a bit younger than me (this was before the whole Demi–Ashton cougar revolution), and with both of us running with different contingencies of the local Irish crowd, our paths rarely, if ever, crossed.

But he knew me too. It's an Irish thing. You hang around long enough, you'll be known ("Who's your one there?" [insert lilting Irish accent]), whether you want to or not, and you'll figure out who everyone else is, as well. Maybe he'd heard I'd once asked about him. I didn't know. As we chatted away like we were making up for lost time, I puzzled: *What is going on?* There were plenty of other girls in the bar. Of course, either they were ancient boozehags chug-a-lugging their scotch (when they weren't coughing up their smoker's lung), or they were ditzy, tramp-stamped twenty-year-olds doing shots. And Maggie, while very attractive, was no competition, as everyone in there who was Irish knew she was married. By default, that left me. Luckily, I was okay with that.

I mean, Connor could do worse. God knows I was more attractive and pleasant than the old bat sitting at the end of the bar who assaulted anyone who passed by with her scary Marge Simpson voice. Yes, I had that going for me, for sure—that, and it was near closing time. You never can tell what's going to happen come closing time. Anyone remember the semirecent Top 40 hit actually titled "Closing Time"? *"Closing time, one last call for alcohol, finish your whiskey and beer … I know who I want to take me home … I know who I want to take me homeeeee, toniiiii- iiiii-iiight!"* Hey, we all know there's some truth to the lyrics.

Who knew how many Coronas Connor had imbibed. He appeared jovial enough but without a trace of sloppy drunkenness. All in all, the odds of us chatting had been fairly good from the moment I'd stepped inside the bar. Besides, my horoscope had stated romance was a distinct possibility for the weekend. Enough said. I was gonna go with it.

So when Maggie finally whispered in my ear, "I think we're gonna catch a cab home," I promptly answered without hesitation, "I think I'm gonna stay." Mind you, it was way past regulatory closing time by now anyway. O'Hooley's is known to stay open a half an hour to an hour later than other bars just to humor its clientele. Like they needed any more "humoring." I knew I really should've been heading home in a cab myself, but Connor was super cute … and I was coming up on the three-month mark since Ray and I had parted ways. I was due to kiss *someone* soon. And if Connor was game, I wouldn't argue.

Maggie smiled with an arched brow and said, "Okay, talk to you tomorrow."

When they flicked the lights on and began shooing everyone out, Connor guided me out the back door in a boyfriendy sort of way. I didn't mind. I missed the boyfriendy gestures of affection. And I figured the lovely in-depth conversation we'd had for the past hour and a half (whatever it had been about), coupled with his boyish charm, lovely teeth, and fun demeanor, and the fact that he wasn't really an actual stranger, made it okay for him to walk me home … to his place, a handy three blocks away. I'd actually come to that conclusion a Ketel One and soda or two beforehand, but that's neither here nor there.

Before you get worried about me being without my faculties and getting attacked, let me calm your fears. I was not by any means drunk, but I wouldn't drive. I had all my wits about me (no slurring, seeing double, staggering, or hiccuping) but was not about to operate heavy machinery. In a nutshell, there was no real beer-goggling on my part. I clearly knew what I was doing. And so did Connor. Plus, if Connor was a certified creep, Maggie would never have left me alone with him—that was for sure.

However, the next morning, which was really not the next morning but four and a half hours later, I lay wide awake, staring at the ceiling while my head pounded ever so slightly. It wasn't a full-blown hangover but just enough to be bothersome, making me wish I could instantaneously be in my own bed, nursing a Diet Coke and inhaling some curly fries. The combination of alcohol and a lack of sleep does not bode well for me. And apparently, in contrast to what I'd thought earlier, I'd exceeded the necessary limit of drinks. I mean, I remembered everything, but the throbbing of my head was evidence enough that it had sadly been too much.

Connor lay next to me, breathing heavily, à la Darth Vader, oblivious to my pain and mortification. Yes, mortification. I just didn't leave and go off with random guys from bars! Okay, well, I had with Ray a year before, but nothing had happened, aside from slobbering all over each other on a darkened dance floor (yep, still cringing). For God's sake, he'd passed out fully clothed on top of my comforter. Relieved, I'd thrown a blanket over him and fallen asleep.

And before Ray, the last time I'd taken off with somebody from a bar (yes, it was another local Irish bar, which shall remain nameless) was five years before. I know what you're thinking. Yes, he was Irish. I also know what else you're thinking. Yes, I did know him. I'd actually spoken to him quite a few times beforehand. We even had mutual friends. But still ...

So my thoughts were, in this order: *Oh my God, where's my purse?*" Thankfully, it was on the floor, and from what I could see, all things of importance were still in it: phone, wallet, and various lip glosses. And for the record, before you get judgmental, good lip gloss isn't cheap.

Please let us have been born in the same decade. Otherwise, *eewww*, I didn't want to think about the status of my cradle robbing. I could make only a rough estimate of Connor's age. He had a boyish face with a tinge of slight crinkling around the eyes when he smiled, but checking out the back of his sleeping head, I noticed quite a few gray hairs. The gray hair quotient boosted my morale, but only slightly.

I have to go to the bathroom was my next thought, but that was going to have to wait, because my next puzzlement was of utmost importance. *Um, how do I get out of here without waking Connor?* I was certain he wasn't going to ask for my number, and it was best that we skipped the awkward farewell formalities that were sure to come.

It was early enough in the morning, and luckily my outfit was pretty inconspicuous, a black Inhabit zip-up cardigan, black skinny jeans, and a pair of Gap city flats. I could easily pass for someone taking a jaunty morning stroll, as long as no one got close enough to smell the vodka that was probably oozing from my pores or to see the raccoon-like remnants of mascara caked underneath my eyes. I figured I could make the trek home in about twenty-five minutes, no problem. Although I would be getting some exercise, it was pathetic that it was going to be a (very fast) walk of shame.

And then I heard it. It was the sound that no girl ever wants to hear when on the brink of attempting a stealth-like exit from a sleepover. Roommates—yes, plural. I could hear roommates. And it was coming from the kitchen. Yes, the kitchen, from whence we'd entered the apartment hours earlier. Not being given a full tour of the apartment at two in the morning, I had no idea if there was a way to get out, other than the kitchen. Besides traipsing through the darkened kitchen, the only other room I'd visited was the bathroom across the hall.

Although we were on the ground floor, the bedroom window didn't seem a viable option of escape. Who in their right mind would be up at six thirty on a Saturday morning (I mean, besides myself)? I fumed. Well, I couldn't stay there all day, waiting for Connor to wake up. I gently tapped the exposed part of his leg that stuck out from under the comforter.

He stuck his bedhead up and squinted at me. I was hoping the squinting was due to being half-asleep and not because he hadn't a clue who I was. "Hey, where are you going?"

Phew. I let out an inward sigh of relief.

I whispered, "I think I'm gonna take off, so is there another way out besides the kitchen?"

"Oh, hold on, I'll take you home." He swung his legs out of bed and grabbed his jeans off the floor. *Lovely.* He was a gentleman, but I just wanted to disappear, not have him drive me home!

"Oh, no, no, that's okay. I can walk. I just didn't want to go ... out through the kitchen."

"No, no, no, you're not going to walk. I'll take you. Just one minute," he said firmly as he shut the door behind him and went into the kitchen. I strained to hear the muffled talking and was sure I detected a female's voice.

Hmm. Well, I'd seen a girl's T-shirt hanging in the bathroom, and a quick glance while passing the open shower curtain had revealed quite a lot of hair products for just one or even two guys. I hadn't thought much of it, because, well, I'd had a few drinks, and it was after two in the morning. At that point I didn't think it odd to assume that he must have a female roommate or a roommate with a girlfriend who frequented the place enough to hang her laundry in the bathroom. However, I was now hoping the female in question wasn't Connor's girlfriend. Did he even have one? I'd assumed not, since he'd taken to walking me home, but then I assumed a lot of things or didn't, depending on the situation and alcohol consumed.

Once again, I'd failed to ask key questions ahead of time, such as "How old are you?" "Do you have a history of psychotic behavior?" "Are you on drugs?" "Ever been in prison?" "Have any kids?" "Are you by any chance gay?" and "Do you have roommates or a ... girlfriend? And if so, perchance, is your girlfriend *one of your roommates?*"

My mind was clearly awhirl with very bad scenarios, all of them involving a fuming roommate/girlfriend who wanted to kick my ass, right after she kicked Connor's. And then I momentarily came to my senses. If he had a girlfriend who lived here, they'd surely be sharing a room, wouldn't they? And looking around Connor's room, well, it was clear there was no womanly touch to it. The king-size bed, covered with a thin, faded comforter, was shoved against one wall, making it only possible to get out of bed from one side—a fire hazard, no? Well, it could be if you had to hurdle over your sleepmate at any given moment. A plastic bureau set of stackable drawers sat under the window, no framed pictures whatsoever of a female companion of any sort upon it, and a huge piece of exercise equipment sat in the other corner of the room, where it served as a monstrous clothing rack. And that was it. If he had a girlfriend, she sucked at interior design and definitely had no sense of feng shui.

Connor entered the room, putting an end to my musing. He threw on a T-shirt and ushered me out. I noted the kitchen door was shut as we walked through a small living room, furnished quite nicely. In my haste to get out of the place before someone actually came out of the kitchen, I hadn't a chance to really look around for telltale evidence of some kind of girlfriend or clues about his roommates.

A new thought suddenly occurred: Was the kitchen door shut because Connor was thoughtful enough to save me from embarrassment? Or was it shut because his roommate/girlfriend was in the kitchen? Or was he trying to hide me from his roommates, who were friends of his girlfriend and would surely inform her? If you haven't caught on by now, I obsess from the get-go.

And now I had the dreaded drive of shame home. It doesn't matter how old you are, does it? It's still awful. You must make awkward conversation until you reach your destination, and then more awkwardness ensues as you must decide if you are going to linger a bit to see if he'll ask you for your number (if he doesn't, you are thoroughly mortified) or decide if you never want to see him again and, therefore, must make a swift James Bond–like exit (i.e., practically throw yourself from the moving vehicle) in case he decides he'd like your number. That's usually the case, no? If you're not interested, then he will assuredly want your number, according to some sort of weird law of physics or statistics that applies to dating.

We drove through the quiet, tree-lined streets of Burlington, puzzling over those out jogging at such an hour, and then crossed into my neighborhood.

"You live on your own up here, Giuliana?" he asked, his eyes upon the road—a bona fide question to ask on a postsleepover drive home, especially as the farther into my hood we got, the bigger and more intimidating the multimillion-dollar homes became. One would surely wonder how someone my age could afford to live here on my own, unless I was some heiress, which I wasn't. It wasn't silly to wonder if I had a roommate (or even two). And I did … a grumpy eighty-nine-year-old woman.

"Actually, I moved into my grandparents' house. My grandma's eighty-nine, and I moved in to try to help out around the house a bit," I answered lamely, even though it was true.

"But just not on weekends." He winked at me sideways.

"Uh, yeah." I'm pretty sure I blushed sheepishly. Did he think I was out every weekend scouring dingy bars for men and leaving Grandma to fend for her eighty-nine-year-old self? He was so not going to ask for my number. Aside from the fact that he probably thought I was some boozehag bimbo, having a grandma as a roomie is usually not a strong selling point anyway. Before he could even pull into the driveway, I reached into my purse and hit the garage door opener. He looked up in slight horror and asked, "Is your grandma waiting up for you?"

I pulled my hand out of my purse, revealing the door opener. "Garage door opener," I said wryly. There would be no lingering. I smiled and said hastily, "Well, thanks so much for the ride home! Buh-bye!"

I catapulted myself out of the car as he called faintly, "Uh, okay, see you around?"

"Sure, okay." I waved over my shoulder as I hurried up the driveway. I was slightly relieved that while Connor might consider me a tad of a bar bimbo, at least he couldn't label me a lingerer. I hit the garage door opener again as he backed out of the driveway. The door descended, and I thought, *Ah, I'll never see him again.* O'Hooley's was not a place I frequented more than once or twice a year. No, I'd never see him again—that was for sure. It was a shame. *Oh, well.*

Two months passed, and suddenly 'twas the night before Thanksgiving, and, well, I ended up at O'Hooley's again. Okay, so I'd reached my year's quota of O'Hooley's appearances sooner than anticipated, but it had definitely not been planned. I'm not sure what it's like where you live the night before Thanksgiving, but in the hamlet of Burlington, it is tradition that everyone goes out on the (small) town the night before the big day. It's been happening since the dawn of time, or at least since we all got fake IDs.

Back in the day, the meeting bar of choice was never randomly picked. Oh, no, careful investigation was done. Phone calls were made. Yes, people actually *dialed* phones (sometimes even rotary ones) and *talked* to one another. A thorough discussion was had about where to go and who of interest would be there. Mind you, the bar choices were not staggering. It was not rocket science, as there were only about three to four Irish bars and one Mexican cantina in the running. But we treated it like so, since people were known to be in town or just out and you never knew whom you might run into. And it was all about being in the right place with the right people (and avoiding a long line in the process). Not much has changed, except the Mexican cantina is now a Baby Gap, and the Irish bars have been whittled down to two. And we texted.

"Where r we meeting?"

"Heading 2 Doyle's @ 9 … K?"

"K, c u then."

Basically, whether you felt like it or not, you were most likely going out the night before Thanksgiving. If you chose to forego the social scene, it could only be for one of these reasons:

1. You are married (happily).
2. You have kids.
3. You have kids *and* are married (happily or maybe not).
4. You don't drink.
5. You are too old. (Sorry, not trying to be ageist. There is some truth to this, the only exceptions being the scary Marge Simpson–voiced lady and her cronies at O'Hooley's or Irish people, as they went out no matter how old they were.)
6. The hangover the next day is just not worth it anymore.
7. You are a complete rebel (or just lame).

I did not fall into any of these categories, although I was dangerously close to being close "old" and was very often lame, but more in the sense of being a complete dork, as my friends liked to lovingly refer to me. Therefore, I was still going out.

My old friend Frankie (when I say "old" I mean we have known each other since kindergarten at St. Dymphna's) was in town from San Diego for the holiday. See, everyone comes home. Normally, I am little wary when Frankie comes to town and wants to go out. Actually, my liver is wary. I love, love, love Frankie to death but know that a night out with him will involve drinking till closing time (usually at O'Hooley's) and then ending up at the local doughnut shop at two thirty. I should mention that when you return home for the holidays, you automatically revert to your college-like antics, hence the binge drinking and early-morning doughnut fests. The plethora of drinks followed by the doughnuts (they must be as good as crack) always seems to be a fabulous idea at the time until you wake up the next day feeling like a complete load—and not just that, but a load who feels like an anvil has been dropped upon your head, as well.

Luckily for my liver, the last few times Frankie's been in town, I've gotten home at a semidecent time, and no doughnuts were ingested. I like to attribute this to the fact that he has been dating a lovely girl whom I absolutely adore. Holly has in no way tried to tame him. Being a clinical psychologist, she's no dummy, and I believe she knows that trying would be a losing battle. Frankie has altered his behavior quite of his own accord. I believe he's in love with the girl. I may be wrong, but it seems to me that people tend to mellow somewhat when in love, and in Frankie's case, that's not a bad thing. So, there's that, and I'd never tell Frankie this, since he'd want to hurt me, but we are unfortunately maturing. Going drink for drink for three or more hours and then inhaling fried and glazed dough just isn't as much fun as it used to be. Or at least the times we do this must be few and far, far between.

So, Frankie, Holly, and I had been at a friend's Thanksgiving party. The annual Thanksgiving eve party is thrown at a mutual friend's clothing boutique. An eclectic group shows up, from those who grew up in the area and went to the local public high school, to those who work in the Starbucks down the block from the boutique. Anyone who's around would surely be at this party. And let me tell you, it's a real hoot when people start drinking and decide to try women's clothes on, especially if they're gay (or supposedly straight) men, but that's another story. After a few hours of festive cocktailing, everyone jovially heads across the street to Doyle's Pub.

However, this year we'd waited a little too long to leave the party and then, to our impatience, found that there was a line down the block outside Doyle's. And let's just say that the people waiting in the line looked quite young. There was no way to peek in and see if anyone remotely close to our age was inside or if we'd look like we'd walked in on an audition for *High School Musical Part 5*. I, for one, just didn't know that I wanted to be jammed in butt to butt with such toddlers.

Yes, as we approach getting older, the bar scene on a night such as Thanksgiving eve is not always so much about who's going to be out. It becomes "How long am I going to have to wait for a drink?" "How many people are going to bump into me, thus spilling my drink or theirs upon me?" and "Am I going to be one of the oldest people in here?" If you are in an Irish bar though, you will probably be spared this last worry by the sixty- to eighty-year-old regulars. We were soon told they were letting in only one person for every one person who was leaving. Upon hearing that, Frankie spoke the words that I was thinking: "I'm too old to wait in lines anymore. Where are we going?"

"Well, O'Hooley's definitely won't have a line. We can cab it there," I suggested with assurance. It was true. There'd be no line and no carding at O'Hooley's. I wondered why half these fake IDers in line hadn't thought of that.

"Perfect, here's a cab," Frankie said, and we hopped in.

Did I think that Connor might be at O'Hooley's? Well, there was a distinct possibility, as it was a good night to go out. But I honestly didn't even know if he hung out there much—another question to which I hadn't thought to find an answer. But the place was a complete dive. If you were going out tonight, you'd be at Doyle's. So, if Connor was out, he'd probably be at Doyle's, and we obviously were not going to be there.

We got out of the cab and walked into O'Hooley's. It was actually a decent night there. The regulars were out in full force, but there were youthful nonalcoholics there, as well. And ... Connor was there. Was this an omen? He stood in the midst of his friends at a table farther down. He didn't see me, which was good. That meant I could sneak sideways glances at him. He was looking as cute as I remembered him to be too. That was also good.

The three of us stood at the bar and ordered a round of drinks. It wasn't long before he noticed me. I knew this because I could slyly see (in the mirror behind the bar) him glancing frequently at me. And he was glancing at me with what appeared to be interest, as opposed to sheer fright. Still, was this going to be weird? Would he come up to me? Which of us would do something first?

I decided there was only one thing to do—go to the bathroom, of course. I actually really had to go too, so it was all perfect timing. Walking to the bathroom would force me to walk right past Connor, and then we'd see what happened. If nothing, well, then I'd have at least accomplished the bathroom trip. I excused myself and made my way down the bar. As I approached, Connor looked up, smiled as if excited and happy to see me, and grabbed me in a tight hug. Well, this was going better than expected, I thought.

"Who ya here with?" he asked, throwing a glance in the direction of Holly and Frankie.

"My friend Frankie and his girlfriend, Holly." Had I overenunciated the word *girlfriend*? I'd tried to throw it in casually.

We exchanged various pleasantries, and I headed off to the bathroom. On my way back, we chatted a few minutes more until I noticed Frankie giving me the eye, and I scurried off. Frankie loves to interrogate me about the current "boys" in my life. As of late, there had been none, much to Frankie's shocked disappointment.

"You always meet guys when I come home. Maybe I should come home more often," Frankie would joke. It was true. He and Holly had been there and witnessed the fateful night I had met and mauled Ray.

However, Frankie was like a brother, and I was just really getting to know Holly, so I wasn't about to tell them that I'd gone home with Connor two months earlier. I mean, I was still getting over the trauma and mortification of the two of them being present for the Ray dance floor hookup. Frankie raised his eyebrows at me and asked, "Who was that?"

"Just an Irish guy," I answered nonchalantly. Frankie stared at me intently for a moment and, when I didn't flinch, said nothing. It was a completely legit answer. We were in an Irish bar, and he knew I was familiar with a lot of the local Irish.

"He's cute," Holly said, glancing over at Connor. "I hope Frankie doesn't put a damper on your mojo!"

"That's never been a problem before." Frankie cackled.

"Ha-ha, shut up," I answered.

We finished our drinks and ordered another round. I sneakily watched Connor in the mirror while he tried to sneakily watch me. His slew of friends took off. I worried that he'd be leaving too. But he didn't. He stayed at his table with one leftover friend. There was still time. For what? I didn't know. I really didn't want to go home with him—at least I didn't think so.

Then Frankie said, "I think we're gonna hit it. I'm kind of tired."

What? It was typical that this would be the one night that Frankie wasn't up for intensive drinking followed by doughnuts.

He continued, "Ready to go? We'll get you into a cab, and then we're going to walk home." Frankie and Holly were staying at Frankie's parents', who lived about a five- to ten-minute walk away. I, on the other hand, lived a good fifteen- to twenty-minute walk from downtown. Trudging home in heels through the nonlit, semisidewalked streets of my neighborhood was never something I felt compelled to do.

"Sure," I answered. I grabbed my purse and looked over at Connor. He was looking directly at me. I waved and mouthed the words "Bye."

He waved back. While I was completely disappointed to have to leave, I was totally opposed to staying in a bar and drinking by myself. If I had one rule (and I had only one rule) about drinking, it was that. Absolutely no drinking alone at home or in bars. It could only lead to trouble.

If I drank at home I'd surely turn maudlin, crying about my age and the fact that I lived at Grandma's, or else I'd continuously raid Grandma's stash of crappy food in the cabinets and the freezer and end up weighing five hundred pounds. If I drank alone in bars I'd be one step away from becoming a boozy cougar or "Marge" at the end of the bar. I mean, the only other things I'd need to fit the Marge bill were some sort of bad perm or dye job and a habit of chain-smoking. I felt my life (at times) was pathetic enough.

And wouldn't you know, we stepped out of the bar, and there was a cab waiting at the curb. Yes, just for me. There'd be no loitering outside the bar in hopes that a certain someone might see me and come out. I thought, once again, that perhaps this was an omen. Why push it? It was clearly time to go home. I sat in the backseat of the cab while the cabbie took a call. Oh, but this was a complete disappointment. I couldn't help but think that if only someone I knew was in the bar, I'd have a legitimate excuse to go back into O'Hooley's, like I had a reason to be there and talk to Connor.

As if on cue, up strolled partygoers who'd been at the Thanksgiving eve shindig. Obviously they hadn't wanted to wait in line at Doyle's either. I knew this, because they were my age. Nobody my age would wait in line at Doyle's. And even better, they were females, and I actually knew them. This was my ticket back into the bar. And Connor was going to ask for my number. Yep, I was going to push it. Why couldn't I just go home and go to sleep? Why couldn't I ever just let things be? And I had the audacity to wonder why, in regard to my love life, random shit happened to me all the time. It was becoming clearer that I was an instigator (or at least a semi-instigator), a shit disturber of love, or something. And then again, maybe it was meant to be. Why would two people I knew just suddenly show up, thus making it plausible for me to go back into the bar? Come on, what were the odds?

Before I could confuse myself anymore, I said hastily, "Sorry, I'm not leaving after all. Uh, here's two dollars!" I jumped out of the cab and followed the girls into the bar. I admit I used the unsuspecting two for my own selfish purposes. Oblivious to me, the two gals stood at the bar, and I hovered casually behind them, as if with them. Connor was now at the bar and, seeing me, waved me over.

"You're back! I thought you were leaving," he said with a surprised smile. Could he see through me?

"I was, but some other friends just showed up," I shamelessly fibbed. Never mind that I had no intention of talking to my supposed friends, who had no idea I was even in the bar. What was the matter with me? Was I desperate? No, I actually wasn't. As I've mentioned before, it's just so rare that I find someone who's physically attractive to me with a personality I like. Being Irish didn't hurt either. What can I say? I'm a sucker for someone funny who also has an accent. And I was determined that Connor ask for my number. Whatever he did with it after that was his choice. But he must at least ask for it and have it in his possession.

"Let me get you a drink, Giuliana," he said.

"Oh, just a water," I said. I'd had enough to drink. I might've pushed it by coming back into the bar, but I didn't need to cross the drink threshold.

Connor tilted his head at me and said definitively, "I can't order a water at the bar. What'll you have?"

I hesitated. "Vodka soda … and a water. Thank you." Try as I might, I never could seem to not drink in O'Hooley's, no matter how hard I tried. I gave myself points for the water, though. Hydration was key.

Drinks arrived, and before I could take a sip, Connor shook his head earnestly and then asked, "So … why didn't I get your number?"

I joked, "Well, seeing as how I practically threw myself out of your truck probably made it a little difficult."

He laughed. "Yeah, you did make a jump for it. Why?"

I grimaced slightly. Now I had to give the standard spiel about how I was completely embarrassed and that I just wasn't "that kind of girl" who went home with guys at the drop of a hat. What must he think of me? Yes, I'd given that speech before, but in my defense, it had been a long time since. It was a speech intended to squelch any belief on Connor's part that I was some kind of brazen minx who haunted dive bars looking for prey. Or at least, if I was a brazen minx, it was only on special occasions. So I gave the spiel, except I inserted the word combo "bimbo-boozehag" for brazen minx—less wordy and more appropriately vernacular, I thought.

Connor listened and shook his head, throwing in gratuitous comments. "No, no, you're not, you're not … oh, no, no, I wouldn't think that."

I appreciated his lying. I wanted to believe him too. Then again, maybe he wasn't lying. Maybe he thought I was a nice girl who just happened to have some fun one night, and he'd been the lucky recipient. But whether or not he was lying, what the hell did he care anyway? Hadn't he had his fun too? Why did the woman always have to take the bad rap for these types of indiscretions? It took two to tango! Yes, yes, it did, but I still wanted him to think I was a nice girl. Because, really, I was, and I am.

That's why when they flicked the lights at closing time, it made no sense that I let him walk me home (to his place) again. I knew better, but it was still happening. As he jokingly said, his arm around me, "I wanna go to Grandma's house!"

I couldn't help but laugh. *Uh, no*, and I told him just that and then changed the subject. "So, who are your roommates?" If they were Irish, I would probably know them, and who was the mystery woman/ roommate anyway?

"I don't have any roommates." He stuck out his lip in a mock pout.

"Right, so *who* are your roommates?" I persisted. *Really?* I wasn't a complete moron.

"I don't have any roommates," he said, feigning petulance, as if I were crazy to imagine such a thing.

Right, so that should have been a key turning point in the conversation, correct? Well, apparently not, if you're me. It was one thirty in the morning. I decided to drop it for the time being.

Again, Connor chivalrously insisted on driving me home in the morning. This time, however, I didn't argue, as I was in heels and quite rumpled clothing. I felt a slight sense of relieved peace on the way home. See, I had garnered some pertinent information on this last visit to Connor's. It had nothing to do with his roommates or the phantom female (whoever she was) who I knew was living with him that he didn't want me to know about. I knew how old he was.

Did I come right out and ask him? Of course not, since that would be the most easy and logical thing to do. Oh, no, I did much better than that. With dramatic MacGyver-like flare, I stole a lightning-fast look at his wallet while he was in the bathroom. I was suddenly grateful to my mom for sending me to that horrid speed-reading course in fifth grade. Who knew it'd come in handy one day?

Yes, I know it seems a very bold, rash maneuver on my part. What if Connor had come back into the room while I was perusing his wallet? *Awkward at best.* Yet I knew I'd find what I needed quickly. I admit I know close to nothing about men, but I do know how predictable they are with their wallets. A man will always have his license in full display in the little plastic window of his wallet, since it's quite sensible and handy. And men are mostly sensible and handy (wallet-wise, at least).

So, it turns out Connor and I were actually born within the same decade. And his birthday was only a few days before mine, albeit seven years later, but whatever. At least I wasn't pulling a complete Demi. We were the same zodiac sign, kindred souls separated by a mere seven years ... either that or, at worst, the male version of myself—(even more) immature and a completely neurotic mess, but with an Irish accent. I conveniently sided with the romantic kindred souls ideal and then realized I was getting ahead of myself.

We pulled into the driveway, and I knew that this time I wasn't going to be able to hurl myself from a moving vehicle. I was in heels, and with one false move I'd wind up looking like a stunt double for Chevy Chase. Therefore, Connor had enough time to ask pointedly, "So, Giuliana, what's your number?" He pulled out his phone. Before I could finish reciting it, he interrupted, "Would that be 415 or 650?" Oh, and he even wanted clarification on area code. I did like him for that even more.

"Well, thanks for dropping me off, and happy Thanksgiving!" I said.

"You too. I'll talk to you later," he answered as I closed the door.

And we did. A week later I got a text from him. And so began what became known as "The Great Potato Debate," or if you're Irish, "Da Great Potato Debate."

Him: "Well, Giuliana, did you have a good day celebrating whatever Thanksgiving is about? Killing Indians or something? How was ur dinner?"

Me: "Yes, I thoroughly enjoyed myself, although it had nothing to do with the death of Native Americans. Must get your history straight. How were your potatoes?"

Him: "Potatoes ... I knew I forgot 2 make something for the dinner."

Me: "Potato slacker!"

Him: "It's not like anyone ever died from not having potatoes."

Me: "Ever heard of the Potato Famine? And I thought you were Irish."

Him: "That was a story our parents told us just so we would eat our spuds."

Me: "Really? Well, potato slacking is still unacceptable on Thanksgiving or Native American Death Day as you refer to it."

And this was just the start. Two days later, our texting continued.

Him: "I dozsed off theda other night n never got 2 finish da the great potato debate."

Me: "Oh, I thought maybe I'd insulted u with the potato slacker remark. Sure, I'm up for debating if it involves potatoes."

Him: "The American contribution of da french fryie n da potato chip cannot be considered in da potato debate."

Me: "So are we just discussing the necessity of potatoes for Thanksgiving dinner? And btw, what about tater tots? Are they not included in da debate either?

Him: "Ah yes the tater tot cousin of the french fry, an icon in American cuisine."

Me: "So you're saying no to the beloved tater tot?"

Him: "I will put it 2 u this way ... how would u feel if I showed up at Thanksgiving dinner with a pot full of tater tots?"

Me: "I would probably still eat them because they're TOTS!"

Me: "And no judging me on my tacky love of tots!"

Him: "Ur American. It's ur heritage."

Me: "Tacky? Ha! Maybe, but I think I've won this debate anyway."

Him: "I didn't mean tacky was ur heritage. I meant tater tots were part of ur heritage. But if ur happy with tacky ... :)"

Me: "Thank you for clarifying. Tots are tacky but in a good way. Gee, the next time I see you, I wonder what we'll chat about since we've exhausted potatoes!"

Him: "What's ur stand on peas? :) Don't worry, I'm sure we will have plenty 2 talk about."

Me: "I prefer carrots, but yes, I'd say the conversation possibilities are endless ..."

And this was all in a day's texting ... and then into the night. Out to dinner with friends in the city, I'd checked my phone to find another text from Connor from a few hours earlier.

Him: "Have u come up with any other hot topics we could discuss?"

Having shared a bottle or two of champagne with the girls at dinner,

I went against my better judgement of never committing a TUI (texting under the influence) and replied.

Me: "I ate too much today, so anything but food ..."

Him: "What was the occasion?"

Me: "Had a girls' dinner in the city, fun, a lot of food, etc. Now we're trying to get a cab home and no cabs!"

Him: "I hate that. Why is there never a cab around when you need one?"

Me: "I know! That's why we're having another drink at the bar."

Him: "Sounds like trouble :)"

And the messaging went back and forth until I got back home at around two in the morning. By now I was pretty much hooked. Give me cute *and* funny (the banter was completely entertaining me)—oh, and the whole accent thing—and I was more than a little intrigued. And the fact that he was texting me late Saturday night and into early Sunday morning meant he clearly wasn't with another girl, unless she was completely comatose, and I didn't figure him the type to be into the semiconscious. My first thought was *What is the matter with him?* And my second thought was *Good.* We would see what, if anything, transpired next.

It was a couple of days later. I sat in my classroom while my class rotated between computer and library, when I checked the time on my phone and saw that there was some type of picture text from Connor titled "<Subject: Hot topic/question> - Is this a good look 4 me?" Underneath was a picture of him waist up in a yellow-hooded raincoat. Ah, yes, he worked outside, some kind of carpentry/construction work. It was a tad grainy, what with the slew of rain coming down and an oddly angled shot, since he must have been taking it himself, holding the camera upward, but there he was. He had a serious scowl on his face, but I guessed I would too if I was working outside in crappy weather. But nonetheless, if I zoomed in, I could still make out his manly, rugged jawline. *Wow.* I had never had a guy send me a picture text of himself. Mind you, it was all very G-rated, but still, it was hot. He was hot. My class was due back any moment. I didn't have much time, so I quickly answered.

Me: "Yellow plastic is very becoming on you."

Him: "It's a bit tacky ... lol."

Me: "Did I imply tacky? It'd really be tacky if you were wearing it while eating TATER TOTS!"

Him: "lol- it's an Irish tuxedo."

Me: "Ha! You're funny ... in a good way."

Him: "Thanks ... I think."

Me: "Funny is good, but maybe I should've said comedic?"

Him: "Sorry bout that. Had 2 do some work."

Me: "I had the kids coming back to class then too. Funny how they always seem to come back!"

Him: "What is it with kids these days? When I was in school we never wanted 2 go back 2 class. Maybe it's because ur such a great teacher."

Me: "Yes, of course, that's it ... that, and it was pretty much time to go home so they had to come back to get their backpacks."

Him: "Next time they leave u should superglue their backpacks 2 the floor n sit back n watch them struggle ha ha ha (evil laugh)."

Me: "Good one. I think I'll use my hot glue gun, though. Now that would be entertaining!"

Him: "Ur glue gun is probably good looking but 2 call it HOT is going a little 2 far."

Me: "I believe I meant temperature wise, but what's not hot about girls toting glue guns. Haha!"

Him: "Glue gun cowgirls! Sounds good 2 me."

It was now Wednesday afternoon. The weekend was two days away. While I was thoroughly enjoying the back-and-forth banter, the typical female question lingering in the back of my mind was *Is he going to ask me out?* I decided to conduct a survey, in which I grilled my friends about this latest conundrum, starting with Maggie. After all, she was married to an Irish guy. Maybe she'd be able to crack the foreign-texting code.

"What does this mean?" I shoved my phone under Maggie's nose that afternoon. She held the phone away and then brought it forward and zoomed in on the shot of the rain-slickered Connor.

"Oh, he's in a raincoat. Kinda hard to see his face clearly, the shadow of the hat part ..."

I grabbed the phone away from her. "Yeah, yeah, but what does it *mean*?" I needed answers from someone, someone perhaps who was married and at least understood men *part* of the time.

Maggie laughed. "I don't know!"

"Why is he sending me a picture of himself? What does this mean!?" I persisted.

Sighing (as Maggie does a lot when dealing with me) and with a smile, Maggie answered, "I don't know! He wanted to send you a picture of himself? He's having fun? Stop overanalyzing!"

Before I could interject, Maggie once again read my mind and said, "Does it mean he's going to ask you out? I have no idea. If his texts are annoying you, stop answering him."

"His texts don't annoy me. I find them very funny … It's just that, what's the point now? He could text his friends instead."

"Right, but he's texting *you*. But if it's going to bother you that he continues to text and doesn't ask you out, then I suggest you stop texting him back and be done with him," Maggie said in her annoying, always-right, matter-of-fact way.

"Fine!" I rolled my eyes.

"Hey, don't be mad at me! I'm not the one sending you pictures of myself and not asking you out!" she shouted back.

"Well, that's 'cause you're married," I said as I grabbed my phone and left in a huff.

The next morning before school, I asked my friend/coworker, Christine, what she thought. I felt Christine's honest opinion would prove to be invaluable, since she's a good twelve years younger and would serve as the voice of today's American youth, who practically came out of the womb texting. Christine was also very Match.com savvy and was always dating someone within the age bracket of twenty-four to thirty-eight. She'd have a clue, I thought.

"Look at this." I strolled into Christine's classroom and handed her my phone.

She clapped her hands eagerly, saying, "Ooh, ooh, what did he text now?" I had been keeping Christine abreast daily of my international texting situation. She stopped suddenly after looking at my phone and raised her eyebrows. "Oh, a picture text. Wow …" She squinted at the phone and looked up, saying, "Too bad there's a shadow over part of his face …"

"I know. I swear he really is cute," I added.

"Oh, I know. I believe you! Well, that seems … promising," she said cheerfully. That's one reason I liked Christine. She was always cheerful, but not in an annoying fake way. She then added, "But he hasn't asked you out?"

I rolled my eyes in answer to her question.

"Hmm, I don't get it. Why are boys so weird?" Christine shook her head.

"Well, maybe he's just not interested and wants to be pen pals … via phone."

Christine laughed. "I don't think so! He could easily text his friends instead, *and* he sent a picture of himself. That's gotta mean something!"

"Thank you!" I said.

Christine then furrowed her eyebrows, adding, "So, what's his problem? Is he trying to work his way up to asking you out? It seems like he likes you … This is very strange. I guess, just wait and see what happens?" Poor Christine now looked as confused as I was. This made me feel slightly better and slightly worse too.

Yes, I was beginning to lose confidence that any of my friends understood men any more than I did. Apparently, the age factor was making no difference. Here I was, at the tail end of my thirties, single, and clueless. Then there was Maggie, thirty-two and married, and Christine, twenty-five and dating around. No one seemed to understand what men were really up to. And if we did, well, was there a possibility that maybe we wanted to pretend we didn't? Ignorance is bliss. Of course, I hadn't exhausted all my friends and their opinions. Yes, I've been known to beat a dead horse.

So, my next victim of interrogation was Holly, Frankie's girlfriend. She had recently moved to my neck of the woods to begin a three-year PhD program in clinical psychology. Holly, an avid jogger, and not knowing anyone in the area but me, was looking for a running buddy. She didn't want to be out jogging alone in an unfamiliar place. In constant need of exercise, and of course really liking Holly and having bonded with her over Frankie and doughnuts, I was an instant shoo-in.

On a late afternoon run, I caught her up to speed on Connor and his texts. If anyone could correctly analyze the situation, could interpret the intent behind one's actions (or texts), it would no doubt be a clinical psychologist. Why hadn't I thought of Holly before? I wondered. Well, I had, but I assumed that with all the critical analyzing she was already doing, she might not want to spend her free time doing more of the same. But perhaps my dilemmas could be used as some type of random field research and would one day provide her with ideas for future focus group studies.

I expected Holly's response to include some heavy clinical jargon that would be totally over my head, with the exception of maybe the names Freud and Jung possibly thrown in. But, hey, I was ready for a professional's opinion. *Lay it on me, sister,* I thought. *And then please explain whatever you just said.*

While we huffed and puffed along the reservoir trail, Holly said, "Here's what I think. I am not into playing games with people, but it is necessary at times, at least with guys. There is a game that is being played here. You have something that this guy wants. I mean, obviously he is getting something out of all this texting."

"Well, not a date," I huffed as sarcastically as I could while sucking wind.

"Well, hold on. He is flirting with you. I mean, he's not sexting you or being creepy, but this is flirting. He likes you. So, maybe you just need to withhold what he wants. He wants to hear from you. So, make him wait to hear from you."

"Well, I do usually," I said, *except when we were in the bantering back-and-forth mode, which had been happening quite a bit.*

"Well, make him wait longer. Men are all about the chase. Maybe that'll get him to thinking that he might actually want to talk to you in person instead of waiting to hear from you. And if not, who needs him?"

"Okay," I answered and then added as I slowed to a walk, "Can we stop for a minute? My knee's bothering me."

On Friday afternoon, at 4:31 p.m. (to be exact), I received a text.

Him: "Why do I tell people I can work on Saturdays?"

My purse vibrated as I paid for some ultraexpensive makeup at Nordstrom that I really didn't need. I glanced at the text. *Hmm. Do*

I answer this at all? I didn't know. If I did, surely it would turn into another fifteen texts back and forth (fully entertaining, no doubt), but which would probably lead to a big, fat nothing. Not that I couldn't just be friends with the guy—I did like him. But the texting to no end was getting a bit ridiculous. And on a Friday in the late afternoon?

In my experience (however limited), guys did not text on Friday at all unless you already had plans with them. Otherwise, the Friday afternoon text might be misconstrued as interest in going out sometime over the weekend. No one had told me this. I had come to this conclusion myself. It was usually true. A guy would not ask you out for a first date on a Friday or Saturday. First dates happened during the week. If one person (or the other, I might add) ended up being a total dud, a weekend night had, thus, not been wasted. At least that's what I believed.

I would text, but I would make him wait. And in the four hours I did so, I checked in with a few friends for their opinions. The consensus was text but wait awhile. Of course, Maggie's response was, "Ugh, I wouldn't text him. He's annoying me now for not asking you out. But … if you want to text him do it."

At eight thirty that night, I sent my text.

Me: "Beats me. Temporary insanity or you're an overachiever."

Him: "Or just plain stupid."

Me: "Your words, not mine. Call yourself enterprising!"

Him: "Is that the nice way of saying I'm stupid?"

Me: "Now, now, there's nothing wrong with a little extra work … but WTH were you thinking?!"

Him: "I don't know … I've ruined my weekend. What about you? Any plans?"

Here was the tricky part again. How to answer? This was the dreaded "What are you up to?" question that no one ever knows how to answer.

Me: "Aside from NOT working, not too many plans. My weekends tend to be extremes. Last weekend too busy, this one not much."

Him: "U need 2 find a happy medium."

Me: "I know, would be nice. Your whole weekend can't be ruined, unless you're working on Sunday too!"

Him: "No I have a soccer game Sunday so I won't be going out tomorrow night … just another quiet weekend for me."

Okay, here I was perplexed. Why was he telling me all this? Did he not go out at all if he had a soccer game the next day?

Me: "I'm imagining you holed up at your place, meditating before your game. Do you leave the house at all?! What happens if you need to make a run to the grocery store?!"

Me: "Hmm, perhaps you need to find a happy medium too. Have a good weekend!"

I was done. I couldn't figure him out. He had no plans. I had no plans. We were texting each other back and forth on a Friday night, and it was now almost ten. I was over it.

Him: "U must think I live a sad existence … I'm actually going 2 my friend's house 4 a while … as 4 groceries, I quite often frequent Safeway."

Okay, now I was annoyed. He had made a big deal about doing nothing, when he was really going out. I do not like being confused, and he was confusing me. I fought the urge to text back something rude.

Me: "Sad, no, not at all! However, you're quite the enigma … good night.

And I meant it. I'd never hear from him again. I wondered if he knew what the word enigma meant and then felt badly for thinking that. Oh, he deserved it for being annoying.

Him: "I have no response 2 that so I will just say good nite 2 u 2." The next morning, I got home from a morning run with Christine and Holly to another text. Surprised, I read, "Not sure if I like this enigma stigma."

Three hours later I answered (against my better judgment).

Me: "Well, work on losing it!"

Him: "I just found out yesterday I had it."

Me (another three hours later): "It's not a fatal disease!"

Him: "Haha … maybe not but is it a bad thing?"

Me: "Not necessarily."

Me: ":)"

Him: "So how is ur nite going?"

Him: "What does that mean?"

Me: "Night's good, heading to a friend's Christmas party. And that was a smile. You may have seen people do that … but in person."

Him: "Haven't seen one in person 4 a while."

Me: "That's too bad. Gotta go, and don't worry, there'll be no TUI (texting under the influence) from me tonight."

Him: "U might get some from me. I took ur advice and left my house. At friend's, might stop by Doyle's in a an hour or so."

On Monday, the texting continued.

Him: "How was the xmas party Saturday nite?"

I replied on Tuesday.

Me: "Morning! The party was fun and I won money! How was Doyle's? How did your soccer game go?"

Him: "Morning … Doyle's didn't happen. Had a change of heart n went home. As 4 the soccer game the less said the better. U won money? Where was the party … in Vegas?"

Me: "Ha! Was in Burlington … ever played the game left, right, center? Involves no counting or skill at all, which is the only reason I won."

Him: "Don't think I've played it but if I can win money I will learn. What about luck? Is that not a factor?"

Me: "Yes, it's all about luck, which I usually don't have either. I should've gone straight out and bought a lotto ticket!"

Him: "I'm the same. I wouldn't win an argument but sometimes lady luck shines on me. I usually end up losing it all again."

Me: "Well, this might be the game for you! I almost won twice. I was on fire!"

Him: "Sounds like ur hooked."

Me: "I'm not much of a gambler, but it was fun. We just got back from a marathon 2 hr all-school xmas play practice."

Him: "I can't think of a better way 2 spend 2 hours :/"

Me: "Kids were totally squirming around by the end. Looks like it's going to rain. Hope you're wearing your Irish tuxedo :)"

Him: "It's like American Express. I don't leave home without it."

Me: "Ha! Thank God they're eating outside, so the class doesn't smell like gross food. I really don't hate teaching, just can't wait for vacation!"

Him: "I'm sorry did you say you DON'T hate teaching? I think I need more convincing."

Me: "I know, I sound terrible. It's the best time of the year but the kids act all wired like they're on crack that you can't even appreciate it."

Him: "Sounds stressful. I know I couldn't handle it. Maybe u need something to take ur mind off it."

Was he suggesting a date? Finally? I decided to parlay.

Me: "I think so. Any suggestions?"

At this point, if he responded with suggestions of self-meditation or downing a glass of wine (by myself), it really didn't matter. That was actually the one good thing about texting: the person on the other end wouldn't be able to see my mortified face crumple in embarrassment or witness me throw the phone against the wall in utter annoyance. And at least I would know, finally, where I stood.

Him: "Would u like 2 grab a coffee maybe later on?"

Me: "Sure, sounds good."

Him: "Say Starbucks on Broadway @ 7:30?"

Bingo. It was a go. You'll be happy to know that the coffee date went very well (at least in my opinion). Upon agreeing to the coffee date, I had been thrown into an immediate panic over whether we'd have anything to talk about. We'd already exhausted the topics of potatoes and hot glue. More importantly, though, conversation would no longer be shrouded by dank bars, infused by adult beverages, nor hidden behind witty but timed texts. What if the chemistry had all been a fluke? What if Connor had no game? Worse, what if I had no game?

I worried for nothing. Connor was still completely cute and still funny. Amazingly, I was still cute and still funny. Conversation went well; in fact, Starbucks had to kick us out. Well, we took the hint when they began moving the chairs inside. I admit I was pleasantly surprised that it had been so fun and gone so well. Yes, I was even slightly optimistic, as optimistic as I could possibly let myself get.

And then I never heard from him again. Well, we sent a few texts back and forth the next day, but that was it.

Over the holidays, while in O'Hooley's with a group of friends, I ran into Connor again. He sought me out, as cute and charmingly Irish as ever.

"You haven't texted me at all, Giuliana!" he chided but with a gleam in his glassy eye.

"You haven't texted me either!" I responded.

"I thought you weren't interested!" he sputtered.

What? I'll spare you rest of the evening's conversation. However, I learned later on from other Irish folk that one of Connor's roommates was, in fact, his ex-girlfriend, the girl he'd been seeing on and off for years. *Lovely.* Of course, I couldn't feign shock, since I'd done enough speculating about the mystery female he didn't want me to know about. Yes, perhaps if I quit my teaching job, I'll look into honing my private investigator skills. All in all, it was probably a blessing in disguise, as I realized that it seemed a bit of a shady situation. Who breaks up but still lives with an ex, even if there are other roommates? Were Connor and his ex exes with benefits? It was all very unfortunate, because I liked him.

A few weeks later, I awoke one morning to find a text from Connor (sent at three in the morning). I admit my heart momentarily was aflutter. What could he possibly be texting at three? I was hoping it hadn't been a blatant booty call text (tasteless and disrespectful). Perhaps, instead, he'd realized that he missed me and wanted another chance. Or he'd moved out and away from the ex and was ready to date again. Maybe he just wanted to say hi. Really, the possibilities were endless. With a knot in my stomach, I clicked it and read.

Him: "Mjugjej."

Yes, you read that correctly—an accidental text, a text so stupid that even spell-check had refused to correct it. I'm sure he didn't lock the keypad, was drunk and fumbling around with the phone, and mistakenly sent me a text. I suddenly wished it *had* been a tasteless, completely disrespectful booty call text. I pondered how someone could accidentally shoot off a text at three and thought about all the witty comebacks I could potentially fire back. I then realized that that one text single-handedly summed up all the dating I'd done throughout my thirties: it was random and confusing, and I couldn't understand it at all, nor would I ever be able to figure it out. And I decided I was finally done with all that. Against my typical judgment, I didn't respond. I decided to finally just let something be.

Much Ado about Something or Other

I always wondered why these types of situations and people (yes, those people) happened to me. I mean, there had to be a reason besides providing mild entertainment for my friends. Was there no justice in the world for the downtrodden in love? I was in a constant state of confusion, disillusionment, and unhappiness—and not just in regard to my bizarre love life. It was everything.

I finally had a random epiphany, or rather, someone I knew pointed my epiphany out to me. I usually have to be beaten over the head before I catch onto things. A friend said to me casually, "Do you think you keep meeting these kinds of guys because you, um, drink a lot?"

"What does *that* have to do with anything? I do not go looking for losers," I said emphatically, if not a bit defensively.

"Well, if you're hanging out in a bar till all hours, the people that are in there with you probably have some issues of their own. Of course, you're going to end up meeting some weirdo!" she (almost) yelled.

Hmm. That was ridiculous. Kind of. Maybe. *Hmm.* I hadn't thought of that. Did that make me a loser/weirdo too? Did it take a loser to know a loser? Or just to attract one? I was again bewildered and this time by myself. It took me a few more educational, if not painful, years to figure it all out. But that's another story altogether.